HADRIAN'S WALL
from the air

G.D.B. Jones & D.J. Woolliscroft

TEMPUS

First published 2001

PUBLISHED IN THE UNITED KINGDOM BY:

Tempus Publishing Ltd
The Mill, Brimscombe Port
Stroud, Gloucestershire GL5 2QG
www.tempus-publishing.com

British Library Cataloguing in Publication Data.
A catalogue record for this book is available from the British Library.

ISBN 0 7524 1946 3

Typesetting and origination by Tempus Publishing.
PRINTED AND BOUND IN GREAT BRITAIN

Contents

List of illustrations   4

Preface   7

Acknowledgements   9

1   Introduction   11

2   Before the Wall: the Stanegate frontier   21

3   Hadrian's Wall   75

4   The outposts and coastal defences   121

5   Postscript   145

Appendix: The anatomy of a Roman fort   147

Bibliography   152

Useful websites   156

Index   157

List of illustrations

Text figures

1   Ditches at the north-eastern corner of Ardoch Roman fort
2   Dalswinton fort, from the air
3   A Cessna 172, four-seater, high wing aircraft preparing for take off
4   Roman northern Scotland in the Flavian period
5   The Roman Gask frontier
6   The Gask tower of Muir O' Fauld
7   Roman watchtowers as depicted on Trajan's Column
8   Map of Late Flavian Scotland
9   The Stanegate system
10   Washing Well, Whickham fort
11   Corbridge, showing Dere Street as a scorch mark
12   Newbrough Sitgate from the south-west
13   Newbrough Sitgate: plan
14   Barcombe Watchtower and hillfort from the north-east
15   Map of the environs of Vindolanda, showing both Barcombe watchtowers
16   Haltwhistle Burn fortlet from the south-east
17   Haltwhistle Burn fortlet excavation plan
18   Carvoran possible early phase, from the north-west
19   Carvoran, plan of the possible air photographic features
20   The Thirwall Gap from the south, with Glenwhelt Leazes temporary camp
21   Throp fortlet from the south-east
22   Nether Denton fort from the south-east
23   Plan of the aerial evidence for Nether Denton fort and *vicus*
24   Nether Denton fort *vicus* from the south-east
25   Mains Rigg tower from the south-east
26   Castle Hill Boothby fortlet from the north-east
27   Old Church Brampton fort, excavation plan
28   Carlisle, the area of the Roman fort and town, from the north-west
29   Plan of Carlisle Roman fort and town
30   Burgh-by-Sands fort I from the south
31   Burgh-by-Sands III from the south-east
32   Map of Roman and native sites around Burgh-by-Sands
33   Kirkbride fort from the west
34   Kirkbride fort and possible compound from the south
35   Plan of Kirkbride and its surroundings
36   The Roman running ditch on Fingland Rigg cutting a native farmstead

37 The Roman running ditch on Farhill
38 Map of the western Stanegate and Cumberland Coast
39 The Roman tower at Gamelsby from the north-west
40 Old Carlisle from the east
41 Plan of Old Carlisle and its surroundings
42 Map of Hadrian's Wall
43 Hadrian's Wall with milecastle 42 from the west, with the Vallum to the rear
44 Map of the Antonine Wall
45 The Antonine Wall milefortlet at Duntocher from the north-west
46 The Antonine Wall fort of Rough Castle from the west
47 Hadrian's Wall east of Limestone Corner from the south-east
48 Newcastle The bridges with the Roman fort area beyond, from the south
49 Rudchester from the north-west
50 Dere Street just north of Hadrian's Wall from the south
51 Limestone Corner from the east
52 Housesteads and the Knag Burn gate from the south-east
53 Milecastle 38 from the south
54 Milecastle 40 from the north
55 The Peel Gap tower from the north-east
56 Haltwhistle Common from the east
57 Cawfields from the north
58 Map of the Milking Gap settlement and its surroundings
59 Possible native sites on Winshields from the south-east
60 The Great Chesters aqueduct from the south
61 A newly discovered temporary camp at Great Chesters, from the north-east
62 Roman style tombs near Great Chesters, from the south
63 Milecastle 45 from the north
64 Turret 48b from the south
65 Milecastle 49 with Birdoswald fort behind, from the north-east
66 The western Turf Wall and Stone Wall junction from the west
67 Castlesteads fort site from the north
68 McLauchlan's map of Castlesteads
69 Stanwix and Carlisle from the north
70 Bowness on Solway from the north-east
71 Knockcross camp from the north
72 Roman north-west England
73 The coastal defences on the Cardurnock Peninsular
74 Milefortlet 1 with running ditches, from the south-west
75 Tower 2b from the south-west
76 Milefortlet 5 from the south-west
77 Milefortlet 9 from the west
78 Silloth playing field from the south
79 Beckfoot fort from the west
80 Beckfoot and its surroundings from the west
81 Milefortlet 17 from the west
82 Milefortlet 23 from the south-west

83   Maryport fort from the north-east
84   Moresby fort from the south
85   Hadrian's Wall: The western outpost system
86   Hadrian's Wall: The eastern outpost system
87   High Rochester fort from the north-east
88   Bewcastle fort, excavation plan
89   Barron's Pike tower, elevated view, from the south
90   Burnswark hillfort with its surrounding siege works, from the south-west
91   A typical Roman fort plan
92   A clavicula style temporary camp gate at Stracathro, Angus

Colour plates

1   Ardoch Roman fort from the air
2   Kaims Castle fortlet
3   Cargill Roman fortlet Perthshire
4   Corbridge from the south-east
5   Warden Hill Iron Age hillfort from the south-east
6   Vindolanda from the south-east
7   Carvoran from the north
8   Old Church Brampton fort from the north-west
9   Burgh-by-Sands fort I from the north-west
10   Milecastle 48 from the south-west
11   Turret 35a from the north
12   Chesters bridge and baths from the north-east
13   South Shields fort from the north-east
14   South Shields fort gate reconstruction from the west
15   Wallsend fort from the south-east
16   Halton Chesters from the north-east
17   Chesters fort from the east
18   Chesters fort baths, from the south-east
19   Milecastle 29 from the north-east
20   Carrawburgh fort from the north
21   Milecastle 35 from the north
22   Housesteads from the south
23   Housesteads from the north-east
24   Milecastle 37 from the north-west
25   Milecastle 42 from the north-east
26   Milking Gap native farmstead from the north-west with the Vallum beyond
27   Great Chesters from the north
28   Willowford Roman bridge and milecastle 49 from the north-east
29   Birdoswald fort from the south
30   Risingham fort from the north-east
31   Bewcastle fort from the north
32   Birrens fort from the south-east

Preface

Hadrian's Wall is one of the best known archaeological monuments in Britain and is now recognised by UNESCO as a World Heritage site. Its remains are probably the best preserved and most intensively studied of their kind anywhere, and much has been written about it at both academic and more popular levels. Until now, however, there has not been a book on the substantial contribution made to Wall studies by aerial photography. Yet the size of the Wall, coupled to the varied level of survival of the actual remains, can make it difficult to appreciate fully the system as a whole on the surface, so that in many ways it is from an aerial viewpoint that one can best understand both the frontier itself and the myriad native and civilian remains which formed the context in which the Wall was built and operated. Many features visible on the ground are better understood in aerial views. Indeed, away from the central sector, particularly on the western side, many of the remains are only observable at all in the form of crop marks and other tenuous effects from above. Considerable numbers of new sites have been discovered from the air and, as many of these have never been excavated or otherwise studied on the ground, the aerial evidence is often all that we have. This book thus offers a new perspective for all those interested in the archaeology and evolution of the Roman Tyne-Solway frontier, which both compliments and supplements that gained from conventional archaeology.

The book was not originally intended as a collaboration and only became so with the tragic and untimely death of Barri Jones in 1999. Prof. Jones had spent much of his working life as an aerial archaeologist. He had a long-standing interest in the evolution of Hadrian's Wall and especially the emerging pre-Wall defences on the western side of the Roman line, in Cumbria, many of which were his own discoveries. He had already produced a short booklet, also called *Hadrian's Wall from the air*, in 1975, but in the mid-1990s the preparation of an exhibition of his aerial photographs of the Wall inspired him to produce a full length book on the subject. Sadly, at the time of his death, only about a quarter of the text and three quarters of the photographs had been prepared and I stepped into the breach to finish the work.

Completing this book has been a process of almost filial affection for me. I knew Barri for over 15 years, firstly whilst a young photographer working in his department in Manchester, then as his student at both undergraduate and Ph.D levels and eventually as a colleague and friend. During that time he constantly nurtured my own growing interest in Roman frontiers, including Hadrian's Wall, and it was with him that I founded 'The Roman Gask Project' in 1995. This organisation, of which I am currently director, is dedicated to studying Rome's very earliest land frontier, which lies on and around the Gask Ridge in Perthshire. In many ways this system was the direct ancestor of Hadrian's Wall and

Barri was to remain an enthusiastic member of the project's steering committee until his death. His infectious enthusiasm also drew me first to the potential of aerial photography as an archaeological tool and then to the actuality of archaeological flying. To anyone used to the calm routine of passenger flights in a large jetliner, low level work in light aircraft can come as something of a shock. My wife came close to the mark when she commented that 'They don't so much fly as flutter'. The planes shudder and jump with each small air current. They often take off and land on rough grass air strips and the photography itself often requires vigorous manoeuvring and tight turns, with the aircraft banked over almost on its side to gain the correct angle on the target. Scratched perspex aircraft windows do nothing for optical quality so the photographs are generally taken through an open window, or even with the door physically removed, and with the photographer leaning out into the howling gale produced by both the propeller wash and the aircraft's own speed. The noise is such that one can only communicate with the pilot through a head set, even when sitting next to him, and the cramped and bumpy environment turns what are usually simple procedures, such as changing a film, into major challenges. It is not a job for the faint-hearted and I would be the first to admit to abject cowardice when Barri encouraged me to take my own initial faltering steps into the air. He himself was utterly fearless, flying in minuscule aircraft, such as motorised hang gliders (which I still will not go near), often in far from ideal conditions. One of my memories from my undergraduate years was a postcard of an antique biplane pinned to the notice board outside his office door. The aircraft was flying almost upside down and on it someone had drawn a speech bubble with the words 'Is this the right angle for you Barri? . . . Barri?!!' Somehow it summed up his approach. He also devised a unique method of low level air photography all of his own, in the form of a heavy lift kite up whose cable a remote control camera could be hauled to take pictures from anything up to around 500ft. This Heath Robinson device was surprisingly effective: I have seen it lift the rear wheels of a Land Rover off the ground during an unexpected gust of wind and it allowed him to take useful air photographs in a wide range of places including some, such as southern Libya, where legal restrictions make normal air photographic flying impossible.

Like many of his former students, I owe him a debt that can never be repaid and, although I would have much preferred that he was still with us to finish it himself, it has been an honour to collaborate on this book. I can only hope that he would have supported the approach I have taken and approved of the final result.

David Woolliscroft, 2001

Acknowledgements

The authors would like to thank the following for their help and advice during the production of this book: Mrs E. Ansell, Dr P.S. Austen, Mr R.L. Bellhouse, Mr B. Berry, Mr I. and Dr R. Bewley, Prof. A.R. Birley, Mr R. Birley, Prof. D.J. Breeze, Mr and Mrs D. and J. Britton, Cambridge Air Photography, The Cumbrian Aero Club, Mr G. Dixon, Dr B. Dobson, Ms P. Faulkner, Mr W.H. Fuller, Mrs S. Hazlehurst, Dr N.J. Higham, Dr B. Hoffmann, Dr T. Gates, Ilford (UK) Ltd, Dr N.J. Lockett, Mr K. Maude, Mr G.S. Maxwell, Prof. N. McCord, The Ministry of Defence, Mr D. Nobel, Mr D. Ridley, Prof. J.K. St Joseph, Mr A. Savage, Mr R. Selkirk, Dr D. Shotter and Dr J.P. Wild.

1 Introduction

Why air photography?

Elevated photography is now a familiar and widely used tool in many areas of research and has entered the public consciousness to influence significantly our view of our place in the world. Satellite imagery and ultimately, of course, images of our Earth from the moon, have revolutionised our view of life on this planet and can now be seen to have fundamentally fuelled the birth of the environmental movement. The advent of air photography in the twentieth century, and especially in the years since the Second World War, has also revolutionised archaeology, both in our understanding of known sites and their surroundings and, still more so, in giving us an unparalleled tool for searching for new sites. Indeed it would probably not be an exaggeration to say that more new sites have been found from the air over the last 50 years than by every other method combined. But what is so magical about aircraft that makes them so effective in this field? The answer, for the most part, is that it is a simple matter of perspective. It is often said by archaeologists that things can be seen from the air which are invisible on the ground. Technically this is incorrect; the surface observer can see everything that can be seen from an aircraft, but, and this is fundamental, not necessarily all at once. All that the aircraft does in lifting us away from the ground is give us a little distance and thus allow us to see the wood from the trees. In other words, it allows us to see and make sense of patterns which, although visible, might be incomprehensible on the surface. We have probably all seen the game where we are shown extreme close up photographs of everyday objects and asked to identify them, and we know that it can be surprisingly difficult: a clump of bristles on a toothbrush can look just like a container of drinking straws. But as soon as the camera zooms out we know at once what we are really looking at. That is exactly what an aircraft does for the archaeologist. It is so simple, and yet so crucial. Archaeological monuments can often be very large, taking up tens of hectares of land but, at the same time, they may be poorly preserved, so that their appearance on the surface is little more than a few slight humps and bumps which may pass unnoticed. Yet as soon as we see them from the air the pattern becomes clear and we immediately know that we are looking at, say, a Roman camp or the remains of a deserted village. In fact most of us already instinctively understand and seek this effect when we visit archaeological monuments and take photographs. Visitors seek out the high points, from which they will get the best pictures, almost without thinking and occasionally raised viewing platforms are provided to improve things further. Just five or six feet can often make an enormous difference, but 1,000 feet is usually better still.

Figure **1** and **colour plate 1** make this process clear. Figure **1** shows part of what is in fact an extremely well-preserved monument, taken with a very wide angle lens which, if anything, gives a wider field of view than the human eye. Even with such advantages, however, it is difficult to make much out. A series of banks and ditches is visible, but they really do not make a great deal of sense. The features sweep out of view on both sides of the picture, so we can tell that we are not looking at the whole of the site, but of how big it is in total and what form it takes we have no idea. Obviously an observer on the ground would not be restricted to this single view point, but even so it might not be possible to really appreciate the site as a totality; this is especially the case on poorer preserved sites where the remains might only be visible intermittently.

Colour plate 1, on the other hand, shows the same site from an aircraft flying at about 800ft and (although taken on a slightly misty day) it immediately resolves into a Roman fort, in this case the fort of Ardoch in Perthshire (NN 839099), probably the best preserved Roman fort in Scotland. Its complex multi-ditched defences become visible as a coherent whole, surrounding the fort platform itself, and even the faint remains of an early medieval church can be made out in the fort's centre. Figure **1** was taken at the ditch corner at **colour plate 1**'s top centre.

Ardoch is, of course, a well-known site which has been extensively excavated and this photograph does not really tell us anything that we did not already know. But air photography has told us a great deal about the fort's surroundings and, in particular, it has

1   Ditches at the north-eastern corner of Ardoch Roman fort, surface shot. DJW

revealed an impressive series of Roman temporary camps just to the north. It is rare to come across such a well-preserved site, however. Many archaeological monuments have been ploughed down to the extent that they are completely indistinguishable under normal circumstances, either on the ground, or from the air and this is where aerial work really comes into its own. For there are conditions which can render such sites visible and, although again all of the resulting effects can be seen on the surface, the patterns they make are best appreciated from the air. Aircraft also provide other advantages in such circumstances, for these effects are often extremely short lived, so that a site may only remain visible for a matter of days or even hours. At the same time, the conditions that produce them often affect wide areas, so that a lot of ground must be covered in a short time. The very speed of an aircraft helps here, as does its ability to fly in direct lines, rather than following often twisting rural roads. The aerial view also allows a broad swath of land to be scanned on any one pass and its ability to ignore property boundaries, broken ground and other terrestrial constraints (except those imposed by air traffic control) gives it a freedom of manoeuvre unmatched by any other means of transport. Some of the effects looked for by aerial archaeologists are now well known to the public; others are less so, but it is worth taking a brief look at the most important to explain how they work and what they can tell us.

Shadow marks

On occasions, a buried archaeological feature can be so thoroughly obliterated at the surface that the minute ridges and depressions which betray its presence are too faint to be readily identified by even the keenest and most trained eyesight, either on the surface or from the air. However, the low sun just before sunset or just after sunrise casts very long shadows, so that the texture of even the flattest terrain can be thrown into such stark relief that the most minute of undulations are made visible (*see* **47**). A similar effect can sometimes be seen after a light dusting of wind blown snow, which will often reveal tiny surface features as the snow will pick out any ridges it starts to pile up against. Both snow and frost may also melt differentially during a thaw as they will heat up more quickly on a ridge facing the sun than in areas which remain even just fractionally longer in shadow.

Crop marks

In the foothills between the headwaters of the Rivers Neckar and Danube in southern Germany, local farmers in the Lautertal had been puzzled for centuries by the annual appearance in their ripening cereal crops of two parallel lines of greener, taller corn. Immediately to one side regular round green patches were also visible in the corn. The local people explained the phenomenon by the fable of a fairy queen who had rushed away in her huge chariot from the scene of a quarrel between her sons. The two greener lines, they said, were the tracks of her chariot wheels, whilst the equally spaced round patches represented a line of hoof marks left by her giant steeds. More recently, scientists claimed that the marks represented a geological feature. But the true explanation emerged when a Roman fortlet was discovered from the air alongside the double line, which itself was shown, in reality, to run between the southern end of the Neckar valley (up which ran the initial version of the Roman frontier east of the Rhine) and the upper Danube frontier.

2   *Dalswinton fort, from the air*

Recent excavations of the crop marks have confirmed the presence of the fortlet and have shown that the two lines of greener vegetation reflected two buried ditches. But what of the 'hoof marks', the round patches of taller growth alongside the buried ditches? Each one, in reality, marked the sump where a wooden upright had been set in a palisade at the front of a bank or rampart. A few pieces of pottery from the fortlet suggested that both it and its associated defensive barrier dated to around AD 100. Thus aerial photography not only helped to explain an intriguing legend yet also put on the map a new, but entirely logical, sector of early Roman frontier, predating a better known stone-built successor that developed a little further to the north.

Crop marks such as this are probably the best known of the archaeological effects visible from the air and they can be utterly spectacular, sometimes picking out almost the entire ground plan of an otherwise invisible monument in uncanny detail. A good example of this can be seen in **2**, an air photograph of the Roman fort of Dalswinton in Nithsdale in southern Scotland (NX 933848) where the defensive ditches of the fort itself (arrow 1) together with those of a slightly later contraction (arrow 2) and a number of annexes (arrow 3) are all clearly visible as dark lines in ripening barley (**2**).

The mechanism by which these marks appear is simple. Features such as buried ditches, which have been dug into the subsoil and later filled in, tend to contain a deeper layer of humus and fertile topsoil than the rest of the field. This allows any plant life growing on the surface to put down deeper roots and gain access to a better reservoir of moisture and nutrients, so that the plants will often grow taller. In the moister soil they will also withstand drought conditions better, but they will often tend to ripen slightly later, especially in a dry summer. Seen from the air, therefore, when caught just as the crops are ripening, such features tend to stand out as often faint, but sometimes extremely vivid, green marks in a field of otherwise golden corn. Harder features, such as the buried remains of stone walls, roads, hard standings and building floors, on the other hand, will tend to have dryer shallower soil above them so that here the crop will have shallower roots, fewer nutrients and poorer access to water and may grow shorter to the point of being stunted, or even die off altogether if put under serious draught stress. Certainly the plants will tend to ripen earlier and so such features will often become visible as premature yellow lines, which we call scorch marks (see **colour plate 32**), whilst the rest of the field remains green. The strength of these crop marks varies enormously, depending on the crop and the varying weather patterns of individual years. In a wet summer there may be virtually no effect at all, whereas some very dry summers, such as 1976, have become classic seasons when sites appeared from the air which had been flown over many times but never previously suspected. Likewise, certain crops, especially cereals, but to a lesser extent oil seed rape, show clear crop marks in even an average summer, whereas others, such as pasture grasses, will only produce them in the very driest of years.

The colour differences provided by crop marks are relatively long lived when compared to shadow marks, but they will still generally last for only a matter of days or, at most, weeks. There are, however, two more effects caused by crop marks, which continue to allow us to gain some data from them right up to the point at which the crop is harvested. For example, even when ripened, the crops growing over buried depressions will still tend to be slightly taller and so, just like small bumps in the ground, they can produce shadows in low angled sun light. There is also a curious polarisation effect, especially in barley, where the crop overlying a ditch will tend to reflect sunlight slightly differently than its surroundings. This effect tends to be highly directional and can only be seen from a fairly narrow range of view points and for this reason deliberate archaeological flights will often follow a spiral course towards harvest time, so that the same ground can be seen from as many directions as possible. The effect can sometimes be positively eerie when seen from a circling aircraft, as an apparently featureless field suddenly appears to switch on a highly detailed crop mark (see **colour plate 3**) as a reflective sheen on the barley heads, and then switch it off again just as abruptly 10 or 20 degrees further round the aircraft's orbit.

Soil marks

The same differences in the topsoil that give rise to crop marks can produce visible effects when a field is ploughed. Firstly, the deeper topsoil where features have been cut into the subsoil will tend to retain moisture better than elsewhere and, after ploughing, that extra dampness may make the soil appear darker in a way that produces comprehensible patterns. The soil might also be a slightly different colour, even once it has dried, because ditches tend to collect standing water and generate lush vegetation whilst they are open so that their bottom layers, at least, tend to fill with a darker humic silt. This can stand out clearly against the parent soil, even centuries later, if brought to the surface when the now completely filled in ditch is ploughed.

Other more positive features can also produce soil marks. For example, the buried foundations of a wall can produce a reverse effect, usually via the soil drying more quickly. But plough damage to the remains can also put a higher proportion of stone dust and chippings into the soil, which tends to lighten its colour in a way that can be seen from the air. On occasions this effect can be dramatic. For instance, the complete ground plans of a number of palatial Roman villas found from the air in the Somme valley in France show up with remarkable clarity as ghostly white outlines where material from their chalk foundations has been ploughed into a dark alluvial soil. Old roads tend to produce a similar, if less dramatic, effect when light bands of gravel metalling are ploughed out, so that they can sometimes be followed for many miles from the air at plough time, especially when sunshine follows rain and makes the wet chippings glisten.

The deeper, damper soil over buried ditches and other depressions also tends to heat up and cool down more slowly than the rest of a field, whilst the shallow drier soil over buried roads or walls reacts more quickly. Below the immediate surface, soils tend to change temperature on a slow annual rhythm, rather then quickly with changes in the weather, or over the 24 hour day/night cycle. This means that in autumn and early winter the soil over buried ditches tends to be very slightly warmer than its surroundings, with the reverse being true in spring. These differences can sometimes cause a field to thaw differentially after frost or light snow and so again reveal patterns to the **air photog**rapher.

The history of aerial archaeology

One of the first known archaeological discoveries by an airborne camera took place in 1906 when a photograph of Stonehenge, taken in drought conditions from a military balloon, revealed the site's approach avenue as dark lines of healthy grass in an otherwise parched field (Capper 1907). With the rapid growth of aviation during and after the First World War, a number of pilots with archaeological or historical interests began to grasp the potential of the strange surface markings they saw from their aircraft. Soon deliberate aerial archaeological flights began, mostly in Europe but also dramatically in the semiarid lands of the Near East and North Africa. A new branch of research had been born, in whose development the role of a small and disparate group of British and French pioneers was remarkable. In Britain, military flyers such as Squadron Leader G.S.M. Insall and Flight Lieutenants W.E. Purdin and B.T. Hood played a key role. But it was O.G.S. Crawford, the Archaeological Officer of the Ordnance survey, who, in the 1920s, really established air photography as a sub-discipline of the already burgeoning subject of archaeology. Two thousand miles away, meanwhile, the French Jesuit priest Antoine Poidebard was proving the value of aerial photography in a wholly different environment by making highly productive sorties across the Syrian desert east of Damascus. Both Crawford and Poidebard published major innovative studies in the form of *Wessex from the Air* and *La Trace de Rome dans le desért de Syrie* respectively. Moreover, both pioneers found disciples. In Britain, for example, we find figures such as Major G.W.G. Allen, who used the technique to study the rich crop markings of the Thames Valley gravels, and Flight Lieutenant E. Bradley. The latter, as a military flying instructor, was able to continue to make observations in Perthshire during the Second World War and often drew remarkably accurate sketch plans of crop marks from the open cockpit of a Tiger Moth biplane, when wartime shortages put film in short supply. On the French side, meanwhile, Colonel Jean Baradez (1949) applied Poidebard's approach to the southern highlands of Algeria, and almost single-handedly discovered Rome's complex frontier defences along the fringe of the Sahara: a truly vast military system, alongside which Hadrian's Wall is dwarfed.

A second wave of research came after the Second World War, mostly in north-western Europe, with figures such as J.K. St.Joseph, D.N. Riley, G.S. Maxwell and others (including ourselves) in Britain, O. Braasch in Germany and R. Agache in France. Throughout these areas, the pressures of massively expanding urban developments and increasingly destructive, mechanised agricultural practices were rapidly altering the landscape. But the post-war leaders in the field differed from their predecessors in that many, and especially St. Joseph, were able to organise sustained and extensive flying programs in which large areas were observed in a systematic manner, year after year in different crop and lighting conditions. This far more intensive approach paid rich dividends and within a few years it was recognised that the impact of aerial photography had resulted in two slightly different achievements. The first was simply to bring to light a huge explosion of new information, as literally thousands of hitherto unsuspected features came to light. This often allowed sites to be recorded in the nick of time before they were swallowed by development projects, and the detection of sites regarded as being of particular importance could sometimes allow them to be excavated prior to destruction, or occasionally even saved altogether.

The second achievement was to allow us to go at least some way towards transforming the traditional view of the evolution of early landscapes. Aerial archaeology has played a crucial role in shifting the emphasis of archaeology from focusing purely on single important sites to a broader view of site interactions both with each other and with the landscape as a whole. The end result has been an increasingly integrated approach to studying past landscapes through 'remote sensing', the collective term now used for a whole range of prospection techniques in which low level air photography is supplemented by satellite imagery and geophysical techniques such as resistivity and magnetometer surveying. The geophysical approach, in particular, has been a valuable halfway house between aerial work and excavation. It was once a somewhat esoteric and underused aspect of archaeology. But it has recently been brought firmly into the public consciousness by the television series *Time Team*, and its results can often be spectacular, revealing extensive archaeological detail without needing either expensive and destructive excavations or the special light and/or crop conditions under which aerial work is most effective. Nevertheless, air photography retains its unique ability to cover large areas quickly and relatively cheaply, and the entire range of remote sensing techniques remains very much complimentary, rather than competitive.

The sheer volume of new information has, of course, brought its own problems, notably in terms of publication. As the emphasis shifted from individual sites to whole landscapes, so a number of regional studies have appeared designed for the general public, including air photographic surveys of county based areas such as Devon, Yorkshire and Shropshire. There have also been books on specific time periods, such as Frere and

StJoseph's *Roman Britain from the air*. Nevertheless, a great deal still remains to be done and many important air photographic discoveries still languish unpublished and unremarked in a variety of local, national and private collections. The present work hopes to make some contribution here and has an advantage over previous approaches, in that with Hadrian's Wall it looks at just one, albeit vast, monument, dating from a single, if broad, time period and can thus afford the space to go into real detail.

Hadrian's Wall

Like the Great Wall of China, the central sector of Hadrian's Wall can be seen and recognised from a modern airliner flying at an altitude of several thousand metres. This is a measure of the impact that such a massive military undertaking wrought upon the ancient landscape, an impact that has endured wherever it has not been destroyed, either by intensive agriculture or industrial urbanisation. The Wall and its associated installations were an engineering feat without parallel in Britain until the coming of the canals and railways. The Wall passes through a range of changing landscapes, running as it does from the tidal reaches of the Tyne Valley in the east, to the serrated granite scarps of the central Whin Sill, before dropping, via the northern side of the Irthing gorge, to the flatlands around the Solway. As will be seen, its modern context also varies greatly, from the industrialised landscapes of Tyneside, to the limestone moorland scenery of the central sector, to the rich pasture and arable country of the low-lying eskers and mosses of the Solway estuary. In all, the frontier barrier cut an 80-Roman-mile (76 statute miles or 118km) swathe across the north of England. The wealth of physical remains (the curtain wall, milecastles, turrets, Vallum, forts, camps, civilian settlements, bridges and so on) is only matched in the desert conditions of parts of North Africa and the Near East, and in none of these regions has the level of investigation and study yet reached that exercised on Hadrian's Wall. The frontier that produced this wealth of visually intelligible and publicly presented archaeology is understandably seen by the public as the key military initiative of Roman Britain, after the invasion itself, and this is probably true. Yet it does sometimes tend to eclipse, in both the popular and scholarly mind, other important facts, notably that Britain also has Rome's first ever fortified land frontier, in the Gask System in Perthshire, and that a second mural frontier, the Antonine Wall, was built across the Forth-Clyde isthmus by Hadrian's successor, Antoninus Pius.

New discoveries are still being made throughout the line but, perhaps surprisingly, it is in the far west that the majority of new information has emerged over the last few decades of aerial reconnaissance. As we shall see, this western data has been particularly valuable in suggesting ways in which archaeologists might decipher the development of the frontier prior to the construction of the Wall itself, by adding a wholly unsuspected level of complexity to the pre-Wall period. The very fact that such far-reaching new discoveries can still be made on the Wall should serve as a cautionary tale to remind us that we are still far from having a complete picture. It should also, however, act as an exciting omen of the likely potential of other much less studied parts of the Roman world. For if a frontier which has already been the subject of nearly two centuries of detailed research

3   A Cessna 172, four-seater, high wing aircraft preparing for take off. DJW

can still yield major new findings to the airborne camera, similar, if not more exciting, discoveries would be guaranteed if aerial archaeology was permitted on several of Rome's other major frontiers which lie in what are now sadly politically sensitive areas (in particular in parts of Algeria, Libya and the Syrian-Iraqi border). This, though, is a hope for the future and, in the meantime, there remains plenty to do on the Wall. Both of us have been asked at various points in our careers why we still study Hadrian's Wall. Surely, we are asked, we now understand this frontier so thoroughly that there is little more left for us to do. As we hope this book will show, the answer is that the grand old lady still has plenty of surprises left and more than enough detailed investigation is still required to both tax and reward generations of scholars yet to come.

Evidence in camera

The photographs that form this new perspective on Hadrian's Wall are the result of aerial reconnaissance that began in 1974 and continues today. Low-wing light aircraft present difficulties for the air photographer, for the simple reason that the wing obscures the camera's view of the ground (*see* **80**), and so the bulk of the pictures were taken from high wing Cessnas, normally four-seater Cessna 172s (**3**) flying from airfields in the Carlisle and Corbridge areas. In the east, the control zone around Newcastle airport and restrictions over military training zones north of the Wall present some limitations on the scope of reconnaissance and, together with the greater presence of arable land (and thus crop marks) to the west of Brampton this has produced a slight westerly bias in the illustrations. But, as already mentioned, there has anyway been a particularly rich harvest of discoveries to the south of the Solway and along the Cumbrian coast. Photographic recording was undertaken using 35mm or 120 format colour and black and white films, which are filed in the archives of Manunair and The Roman Gask Project, both of the Department of Archaeology, University of Manchester. The photographs were taken by Barri Jones, except where otherwise stated.

2 Before the Wall: the Stanegate frontier

The concept of a frontier

To a Roman of the time of the Emperor Claudius' invasion of Britain in AD 43, the idea of a frontier as a permanent, let alone heavily fortified, line on the ground would have been all but incomprehensible. The Roman Empire had by that time been expanding for centuries to cover an area which stretched from the Atlantic to the Euphrates and from the North Sea to the Sahara and there seemed no real reason why it should not continue to grow. The Augustan poet Virgil had popularised the concept of *imperium sine fine*, or 'Empire without limit', and it did not seem **impossib**le that Roman power would continue its inexorable spread until it covered the entire world. Yet barely more than a generation later the first fortified land frontiers were beginning to appear, and within 80 years vast, complex and apparently permanent systems such as Hadrian's Wall were being built.

Quite why this change occurred is still very much open to debate, for it was essentially an admission of failure, but there are a number of factors which might be discussed. One consideration must surely be the often strained political situation within the Roman Empire itself, at whose very heart lay a dangerous constitutional paradox which was never really solved. To many twenty-first-century minds, Empire and Emperor go together almost without saying, but this was not the case in ancient times. For although the Roman Empire was a monarchy in effect, it always remained in law the semi-democratic republic it had been for centuries before the first of the Emperors, Augustus, began the series of one man regimes in 27 BC. The Republic was believed to have come into being in 510 BC, after the expulsion by force of an ancient and eventually much hated monarchy, and forever after the very word 'King' (in Latin *Rex*) remained a dirty word in Roman politics. As late as the first century BC the republican general and dictator Julius Caesar had been murdered in no small measure because he was believed to be planning to make himself king; this antipathy always remained so strong that, even after centuries of imperial rule, none of the Emperors ever tried to adopt the title. Augustus himself was Caesar's great nephew, but although he came to power through a series of civil wars, he had learned the lessons of his uncle's downfall well enough to apply a little more tact. The result was a constitutional compromise. In reality he was a military dictator with unchallengeable power based on the support of the army. But a scene was stage managed with the original republican ruling assembly, the Senate, in which he ostentatiously laid down his usurped powers and restored the Republic before being appointed to a legitimate, if unusual, combination of traditional republican offices, which he then, ever after, claimed were the only basis for his authority. He was not, therefore, king, but *Princeps*, or first amongst equals. The arrangement was, of course, an out and out fiction and no one can really have been fooled, despite occasional modern claims to the contrary, since the iron hand had been given an extremely thorough public airing before being clothed in its velvet glove. Augustus' real position continued to depend on the military and no amount of republican titles would have saved him (as indeed they failed to save all too many of his successors) had he lost that support, but they did have the advantage of propaganda value in appearing to legitimise his position. The fiction also helped to assuage the dignity of the old republican ruling class, whose military and administrative expertise was still vital to the sound governance of the Empire and, in doing so, it helped to bring peace to a society exhausted by a generation of civil strife. There was, however, one serious flaw, because the entire arrangement was built up to reflect the extraordinary position of a single citizen. It did not create a monarchy, let alone a hereditary monarch. Quite the reverse: it supposedly restored the ancient status quo and, in theory, Augustus held a special position only because he was an exceptionally able statesman who had earned it and when he died, or chose to step down, the normal republican process would continue.

Rome was thus placed in a deeply paradoxical situation. Mann (1974, 509) has put the initial position rather nicely when he says that 'Roman history is essentially the virtually unique story of a nation trying to catch up with the situations produced by the incredible success of its army'. The disastrous instability of the last two generations of the Republic had suggested that government by the old consensual constitution was no longer possible, as again and again senior commanders, culminating in Augustus himself, had been desperately needed to take over ever more powerful military commands, but had then failed to play by the political rules. There appeared, therefore, to be a need for a monarch of some sort and in effect they had created one in Augustus, and yet legally they had not. Augustus was, therefore, the Emperor of an Empire that had no office of Emperor. While he lived, this may not have mattered unduly, but it did mean that there was no legally sanctioned basis for the succession (and never would be). For how could one legislate about the succession to a position which officially did not exist?

Imperial rule had, in fact, come to stay and was to continue unbroken until the fall of the Eastern Empire in 1453, but this issue was never satisfactorily settled, leaving Rome ever after with an unenviable record of military coups and usurpations. Emperors who had come to power through military means were understandably keen to prevent anyone else from following their example and this was to have a profound knock-on effect on the Empire's previous dynamic towards enlargement. Rome had never, from its earliest days, separated military and political career structures and many of the old republican governmental offices, such as the consulship, had both military and administrative functions. At the same time, military success had always been the primary route to status and charisma and increasingly, through war booty, wealth. All of these were vital in a politician's quest to rise up the political ladder and so in the late Republic a great deal of the Empire's expansion had come about on a more or less ad hoc basis as individual generals staged or provoked wars of conquest to further their own position. The charisma of military glory lived on under the Empire and, as the emperors were understandably nervous of allowing anyone else conspicuous military success in case it provided the power base for an attempt on the throne, imperial generals were kept on a very much tighter reign.

Another consideration was bureaucratic. In the old expansionist days, the exact line of the frontier was relatively unimportant. It was anyway likely to be a temporary position and it would often take the form of a broad militarised zone rather than a fixed line on a map. With the arrival of a more static situation, however, various requirements made a more definite situation desirable; the most important of these may have been that Roman revenue officials needed clear limits to their authority in order to know exactly who they could tax.

A third factor is the possibility that the Empire had begun to run up against the law of diminishing returns. There are a number of ancient writers who try to console those Romans who still lusted for world empire by arguing that Rome had conquered everything worth having and was right not to waste blood and resources on profitless barbarian outlands. To some extent this is simply a natural human reaction — sour grapes — to soften the blow of disappointment, but it does have an element of truth. The wealthy civilizations of classical antiquity were concentrated around the Mediterranean basin and this Rome now held in its entirety. The lands beyond were far less developed economically, which meant that their booty and eventual taxes were less likely to pay for the military and administrative expense of conquering and holding them. A variation on this theme is an interesting idea first put forward by W. Groenman van Waateringe (1980) with relation to the Rhineland, and since mentioned in a British context by both Breeze (1988, 13ff) and Millett (1990, 54f and 99f). The Romans generally sought to avoid leaving large numbers of administrators in conquered provinces, at least for any time, and the military presence was also kept to a minimum, especially in areas away from the frontiers. They tended instead to take the local administrative, legal and law enforcement systems largely as they found them and simply turned them to their own ends, under the overall direction of provincial governors and their surprisingly minimal staffs. This often meant that, even after quite bloody wars of conquest, local elites were left with their power and wealth intact and simply acquired responsibilities to the Roman state for taxation and judicial concerns which, in any case, they might already have been discharging under their pre-conquest government. In other words, Rome ruled most of her captive states not by the direct supervision or coercion of their populations, but merely by bending their governing classes to the imperial will; even here, so long as all went well, the Empire frequently seems to have had a fairly light touch. The deal was also reciprocal, often to the point of symbiosis. The local magnates not only survived; their position necessarily acquired imperial backing. They continued to run their communities, albeit on Rome's behalf, and they could profit from doing so well, not only by preserving their local status and power but, with time, the more able and ambitious might also now hope for still more profitable careers on the Empire-wide stage. Indeed, through Rome's almost unprecedented generosity with her own citizenship, they could aspire to become legally one of the conquering people, rather than one of the conquered. They thus acquired a vested interest in preserving the imperial power rather than, as might otherwise have been expected, becoming natural focuses for resistance to it.

It was a brilliant system and, on the whole, it worked superbly well. It made efficient use of (and eventually expanded) the meagre pool of Roman manpower. It was cheap to operate. It made local peoples feel less under the imperial thumb and the provincial elites, being small and readily identifiable, were more easily encouraged, suborned, communicated with and, if needs be, intimidated than entire populations. In short, it was a system that allowed Rome to govern an empire by, at least tacit, consent that she would have found it difficult to rule by force alone. The only problem was that it had grown up on the assumption of finding the sort of centralised, Mediterranean city state or kingdom style societies which possessed the necessary political infrastructure to render them capable of being left to run themselves in this way. Unfortunately, Rome had begun to enter areas, especially in northern Europe and North Africa, where this could no longer be relied on. Many of their societies show few archaeological signs of such development and there is little to suggest the existence of any but the most embryonic central authorities. The suggestion could be made, therefore, that the Romans simply found the socio-political state of these areas to be too incompatible with their established system of provincial governance to be either practicable or, at least, cost effective, with the resources they had to hand.

Finally, there were more straightforward military questions. Firstly, a growing knowledge of geography was showing the Romans that the world was a great deal larger than they had initially thought and that the existing Empire, vast as it was, constituted only a small fraction of the whole. The military problems of indefinite expansion on that sort of scale must have been daunting indeed, especially given the limited logistical and communications technology of the time (Woolliscroft 2001). Secondly, in the East, Rome had slowly been forced to accept the fact that, in the Parthian Empire, she had for the first time met a superpower equal to herself. This huge kingdom was the heir to the old Persian Empire of Classical Greek times and stretched from the Euphrates to the borders of India, with its heart lands amongst the still more ancient civilizations of Mesopotamia. Relations between the two had got off to a bad start when Rome tried to treat Parthia as just another minor eastern potentate to be treated with bullying contempt. Worse was to follow when a number of Roman generals tried to crown their careers by conquering the kingdom. Two, Crassus and Mark Anthony, actually mounted campaigns, with almost equally disastrous results, and Julius Caesar himself had been about to leave on another when he was assassinated. The nettle finally had to be grasped that neither Empire was strong enough to assimilate the other and for the most part, during the imperial period, the two lived in a nervous *modus vivendi*, albeit with the occasional serious flare up, with a frontier based on the Euphrates. Elsewhere, frontiers came about almost by default. Augustus, for example had been the greatest expander of the Empire, annexing Egypt, the Danube lands and the few remaining unconquered parts of the Alps and northern Spain. But his attempt to absorb Germany, although initially successful, ended in catastrophe when the governor Varus and his army of three Roman legions were ambushed and all but annihilated near Osnabrück in AD 9. Augustus, by now an old man, lost his nerve and although the northern armies remained on the Rhine and Danube, officially prepared to strike back, these riverine dispositions rapidly fossilised into de facto frontier defences.

Despite these pressures towards imperial constraint, some expansion did take place under Augustus' successors, including the annexation of parts of North Africa and the Near East, which had previously been run as client states, and, perhaps most importantly, the invasion of Britain by Claudius, and Dacia (Romania) by Trajan.

Nevertheless, expansion became the exception rather than the rule. The fact that the Empire had accepted, albeit somewhat absentmindedly, that it had borders, however, in no way determined that it also needed to build massive linear fortifications along the frontier lines, and indeed these did not begin to emerge until the late first century AD. It could, in fact, be argued that such fortified frontiers even weakened, rather than strengthened, imperial defence. For they tended to absorb large amounts of manpower and spread it along the frontier, rather than keeping it concentrated in powerful battle groups. A number of explanations could be offered for why this particular route was taken. Luttwak (1976) has suggested that the Romans were seeking what he calls 'preclusivity'. What this amounts to is that the Roman government wanted to be able to maintain to the ultimate one of its proudest public relations achievements: the so-called Pax Romana, or 'Roman peace'. This was, in effect, a guarantee of total internal peace and security and represented at least the attempt to ensure that any citizen would be safe anywhere on Roman soil. This was important not only as propaganda, popularising imperial rule by giving it an active advantage, but also for political reasons. For the Pax Romana allowed Rome to be the first ever state to disarm its civilian population. The ban on civilian weapons could be justified if citizens could be sure of being protected by the state, but it obviously had the added benefit, from the government's point of view, of making it very much harder to rebel. Once established, the frontiers would also have fed off themselves to some degree, because the logistical needs of their soldiers meant that it was very much in the government's interests to promote (through security) the development of prosperous communities right up to the line itself. Their agricultural and industrial production could then supply the troops and so reduce the need for the expensive long-haul transportation of goods. What all this meant, however, was that the frontiers had to be virtually airtight. They had to protect the Empire not just against full-scale invasion, but also from the smallest of cross border raiding and sheep rustling parties. The fortified lines were functionally far better suited to this policing role and they would also have had considerable propaganda value, for many of these complex systems, and especially Hadrian's Wall, would have been visually very impressive. Their appearance and the very fact that the Romans could build them at all, through often very difficult terrain, must have added to their deterrent value on potential raiders, as well as being reassuring (though still suitably cowing) to borderland provincials. The full potential of this effect can be lost on modern man, used to grandiose engineering projects, although it is still difficult to walk even the ruins of the central sector of Hadrian's Wall without being impressed. But a better idea of their contemporary impact might be looked for in the attitudes of earlier, post-Roman but pre-industrial, ages. For them it seemed impossible that such things could have been built by mere men and it is no coincidence that the Medieval names for both the Antonine Wall in Scotland (*Grymisdyke*) and the Raetian frontier in southern Germany (*Teufelsmauer*) meant Devil's Wall.

There was also a potential taxation benefit to tightly controlling the borders. The Empire's tax base included duties levied on both imports and exports, and the same security measures that were designed to stop illicit frontier crossings could channel more legitimate traffic through recognised control points and ensure that these duties were not evaded. It has been argued too that there may have been political benefits in keeping the army busy, dispersed and far from the centre of power, where its presence, especially if idle, could have been a destabilising factor. Indeed Mann (1974, 532) has gone so far as to describe the entire process of building and operating frontiers as 'displacement activity', i.e. something virtually pointless in itself, but an effective long term method of occupying a powerful and potentially restive section of society.

The frontier in Britain

The decision to build a physical barrier in Britain might be traced to a visit to the province by the Emperor Hadrian in AD 122. This massive undertaking has, however, understandably tended to obscure the evolution of the British frontier during the preceding decades. Roman opinion in the first century AD had expected total conquest of the island. Yet, after the suppression of the initial tribal opposition under the leadership of Caratacus, Rome's military focus lay principally in Wales and the Marches. This strategic disposition depended on a political alliance with the pro-Roman element of the Brigantian tribal confederacy, led by Queen Cartimandua, in what is now northern England. But this precarious alliance was increasingly threatened by an anti-Roman element in the tribe, later led by Cartimandua's husband, Venutius. It did, though, survive the bloody rebellion of Boudicca in the south-east in AD 60, and only fell apart when Cartimandua was deposed during Rome's brief but violent civil wars following the death of the Emperor Nero in AD 68.

The loss of the Brigantian alliance acted to force the emergence of a renewed forward policy under the new Flavian dynasty Emperors (Vespasian and his sons Titus and Domitian) in the AD 70s and early 80s. The governor Cerialis reached at least as far as Carlisle by AD 71 and the fact that this dating derives from dendrochronology (tree ring analysis) of a permanent timber fort on the site (Caruana 1997, 40f, and forthcoming, and Groves 1990) shows that he intended to stay. This dating initially came as a great surprise as it had not been thought that permanent military occupation had stretched this far north before the end of the 70s. But there have been growing suggestions of late that Cerialis may have penetrated much further still, perhaps as far as Perthshire (Caruana 1997, 46f and Shotter 2000, 194f). Meanwhile, the final detailed conquest of Wales had been largely completed by AD 75, and evidence that total conquest of Britain was still being taken for granted at this time can be seen in the eulogy of Agricola, the province's most famous governor, written by his son-in-law, the historian Tacitus. But, although Agricola defeated a Caledonian confederacy at Mons Graupius, somewhere in north-eastern Scotland, in AD 83, the full impact of that victory was quickly nullified by a strategic retrenchment caused by the need to send substantial military reinforcements (amounting to one of Britain's four Roman legions along, no doubt, with auxiliary forces) to the continent following a disastrous series of defeats on the Danube. These forces were never to return.

The Gask frontier

At some point during the 70s or early 80s, Rome's first frontier in Britain was constructed. It ran on and around the Gask Ridge in southern Perthshire, between Doune on the Teith and Bertha on the Tay (**4**), although quite how it fits in with the Agricolan campaigns and their aftermath is currently somewhat uncertain. Until recently, it was thought that the Gask had been occupied only very briefly, perhaps for as little as a single season. The most convincing account of its context (Breeze 1982, 65) had suggested that as the dreams of total conquest faded with the troop withdrawals of the mid 80s, the Romans abandoned a forward line of forts from Drumquhassle to Stracathro (**4**) which may have been intended as a jumping off line for further advances, since it included the legionary fortress of Inchtuthil. They had, however, attempted to hold onto the bulk of what they already had and so built the frontier to protect Fife and the strategic pass of Strathearn. Recent excavations have, though, made this short chronology far more difficult to accept. A number of sites on the system, including four substantial oak watchtowers, had needed rebuilding at least once and possibly twice during their operational lives, which suggests a much longer occupation. Just how long, though, still remains open to question, but it now seems more likely that the frontier's foundation date must be pushed back at least to the beginning of Agricola's activities, if not beyond. Ironically, this re-dating of the Gask frontier to a rather earlier time coincided almost exactly with a German announcement that their frontier, which was once thought to be slightly earlier than the Gask, dated to the reign of the Emperor Trajan, 15-20 years later than had been thought (Körtüm 1998). This means that the Gask now represents the very earliest of Rome's fortified land frontiers.

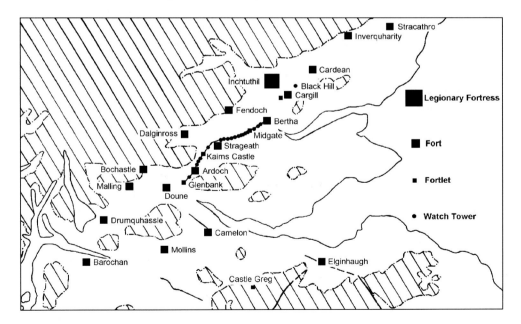

4   *Roman northern Scotland in the Flavian period.* DJW

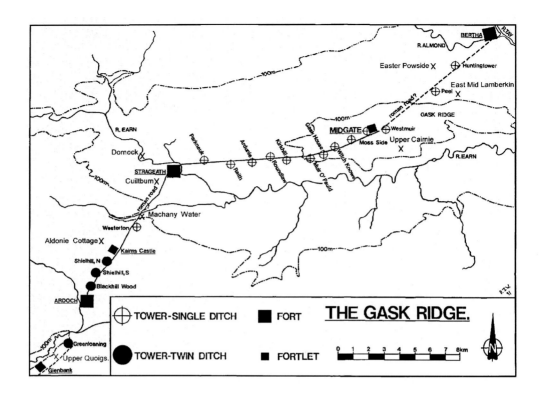

5   *The Roman Gask frontier.* DJW

The system itself consists of a chain of fortifications strung out along the Roman road to the Tay (**4 & 5**) and consists of four basic elements, of which the first is the road itself. This is a classic, well-engineered, all-weather Roman road of between 6 and 8m wide and consists of a rammed gravel surface resting (usually) on a bed of larger stones. In damp areas the entire structure has sometimes been built up on a low turf built bank or *agger*, and it makes occasional use of small cuttings and embankments, especially when crossing stream valleys (although the usual drainage ditches to either side are often lacking). As befits a Roman road, it frequently runs almost perfectly straight for miles at a time and much of it can still be seen. Quite a number of stretches are still in use, as either public roads or farm and forestry tracks. Of the rest, the great bulk has now been traced by air photography, either as parch and soil marks, caused by the structure itself, or as parallel lines of rounded crop marks caused by the small quarry pits from which the building material was dug. For the most part, only short sections still remain to be identified, although the exact line of the last few miles before the Tay has yet to be traced.

    The fortifications consist of a series of turf and timber built forts, smaller fortlets and watchtowers, all of which lie close to, and often right beside, the road. There are three forts on the line: Ardoch (**colour plate 1**), Strageath and Bertha and all three are large (up to 8.6 acres) auxiliary forts, capable of holding at least one complete unit. Only Ardoch has

6   The Gask tower of Muir O' Fauld. DJW

yet produced any evidence to identify its garrison, but this fort has yielded the tombstone of a soldier of *Cohors I Hispanorum* (The First Cohort of Spaniards), apparently dating to the first century AD. This unit is later attested as being 1,000 strong and *equitata* (part mounted). But at Ardoch the cohort seems to have been just 500 strong and its title, as given on the inscription, would suggest a purely infantry unit (Jarrett 1994, 45f).

The fortlets are much smaller installations of around 20m x 22m internally. Three are now known with certainty, at Glenbank, Kaims Castle and Midgate, with one more suspected at Raith, and they may occur at a fairly regular spacing interval of six Roman miles (8.87km). **Colour plate 2** shows an aerial view of Kaims Castle (NN 861129), the best preserved of the three, and it is fairly easy to see the almost square internal area, surrounded first by a turf rampart and then by a ditch. Both defence circuits have a single entrance break facing towards the Roman road, which is itself faintly visible as a slight rise running from left to right immediately in front of the cottage garden fence visible in the top left-hand corner of the photograph. All three of the known Gask fortlets have now been excavated (one, Glenbank, by the second author), and all have produced something of a mystery. For none of them have shown signs of internal buildings, whereas one would normally expect to find at least a single and often a pair of barrack blocks fronting onto a central roadway. It would seem, therefore, that the Gask fortlets were either highly unusual and simply never had internal buildings or, perhaps more probably, that their buildings are for some reason no longer archaeologically detectable. Perhaps they were of

7   *Roman watchtowers as depicted on Trajan's Column.* DJW

mud brick, cob or turf walled construction or they may have been founded on sleeper beams, which rested on, rather than cutting into, the surface. Possibly even tenting was used for seasonal occupation, but whatever the case their remains may have been destroyed long ago.

The smallest and most common site type on the system are the towers. Eighteen are known at present and there are almost certainly several more still awaiting discovery. These were simple timber structures, perhaps originally around 10m high, and were founded on four large timber corner posts. They were surrounded by a low turf rampart and then by circular to sub-rectangular ring ditches, again with single entrance breaks facing the Roman road. Their entire diameter is generally less than 25m, with the towers themselves 4-5m square. They presumably acted as observation posts, although they probably also had a signalling capability, and Roman artistic representations, such as the opening scenes of Trajan's column (**7**), show similar towers with pyramidal roofs and elevated balconies, presumably to act as observation decks. But although the ground plans of many of the Gask towers have now been excavated, we have little evidence with which to reconstruct their superstructures, except that they seem to have had wattle and daub side cladding. Figure **6** shows the tower of Muir O' Fauld (NN 982190), one of the few well-preserved examples not to be obscured from the air by woodland. The site is visible as a single ring ditch preserved in a clearing and it is fairly typical of the towers as a whole, although the sites to the south of Kaims Castle (including the southernmost fortlet, Glenbank) have a second ditch. The modern forestry track, which runs diagonally across the top of the picture, follows the line of the Roman road, and the tower's single entrance causeway is faintly visible facing it, roughly at the ditch circuit's 11 o'clock position.

If the starting date and exact life span of the Gask frontier is now uncertain, its abandonment can be dated with more confidence, and current theory rests largely on Hobley's (1989) analysis of the coins from northern Scotland. Roman first-century coinage did not enter Britain in a steady flow. Instead, new coins were only provided by the central mint when they were needed for some reason, perhaps to top up a government pool usually reliant on the province's own taxation. There are thus 'surge' years when large numbers of coins arrived, followed by dearth periods (which could last for many years) when new coins were rare and probably only entered through trade and other non-governmental processes. AD 86 and 87 were particular surge years, so much so that it is unusual for a site of any significance occupied during those years not to produce their coins. There was then a pause in the coin supply, which lasted until after the death of Domitian in 96. Northern Scotland has produced a number of coins of 86, including one from the Gask fort of Strageath, and an unusually high percentage of these are found in mint or near mint condition. None are known with certainty from 87, however. Under these circumstances, the absence of 87 coins would suggest that the Gask went out of use at some time after the coinage of 86 arrived in the province, but before the arrival of coins of 87, which might be expected to be well into that year. At first sight this does appear to be a convincing argument. It coincides well with the time of the troop withdrawals and it may well prove to be right, but it does still have small weaknesses. In particular, only 11 coins of AD 86 are known from military sites north of the Forth-Clyde isthmus, which might not be enough to be statistically significant, especially as the identity of one of the coins is disputed. Whatever the case, it should be remembered that a single firmly dated coin of 87 would have the potential to extend the occupation of the Gask, not by a single year, but by the decade which elapsed before coins arrived in bulk again at the start of the reign of Nerva. More realistically, it would certainly allow us to extend the occupation until around AD 90, after which the pottery finds also cease to take us further (Hartley 1972).

Whatever its exact life span, there has long been evidence to suggest that when the Gask system was eventually abandoned this was a matter of deliberate Roman policy rather than the result of, at least direct, native coercion. For there is no evidence for the sort of destruction we might expect from hostile action. Instead, we find a picture of careful demolition and the removal, destruction or burial of any material likely to be of use to an enemy. The Roman Gask Project's work has recently added further support to this picture. Glenbank had its gate tower posts dug out. Midgate had its ramparts partly shovelled into its ditch and, at both Greenloaning and Shielhill South, the tower posts had been dug out and burned, along with the wattle and daub panelling, at the end of the second structural period. But we can introduce one subtle extra nuance, for although the end when it came may well have been orderly, it might also have been rather sudden and unexpected by the men on the ground. The evidence for this lies in Midgate's apparent abandonment part way through having its ditch re-cut: not, one would have thought, a particularly long job on a site of this size, and something that would surely not even have been started had the garrison known that they were about to leave.

It used to be thought that the withdrawal, even from the Gask line, might have been a relatively gradual, phased affair, but Hobley's coin analysis would suggest that the Romans actually pulled right back to behind the Southern Uplands in one fell swoop. With the possible exception of Loudon Hill fort (**8**), no coins of 87 are met with on Roman military installations until quite far south along Nithsdale, Annandale and Dere Street. The northernmost limit of Roman occupation thus came to rest on forts such as Dalswinton (**2**) and Milton in the West, and Newstead in the East. Seen on a map, these may appear to form a relatively coherent line. But they were separated by mountains and cannot really be called a frontier in the sense of an organised disposition of military forces along a defensive perimeter, whether or not demarcated by a fortified barrier. They were simply the northernmost occupied points on the main Roman routes into Scotland. There was certainly no ancillary chain of fortlets and watchtowers and no direct east-west running road to link them together. Instead, the next 30 years saw the gradual development of a new frontier a little to the south, on the Tyne-Solway isthmus, and virtually everything north of that line had been given up by around 105.

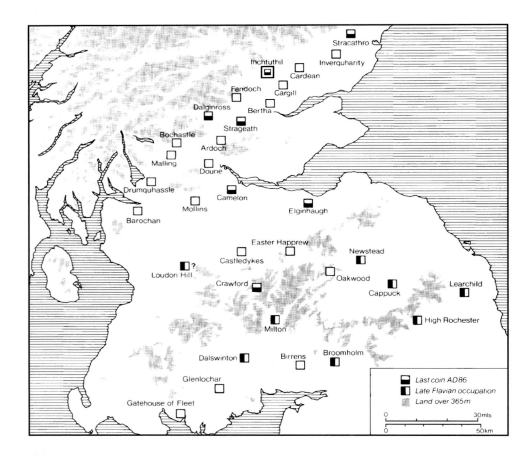

8   *Map of Late Flavian Scotland.* Reproduced by kind permission of A.S. Hobley

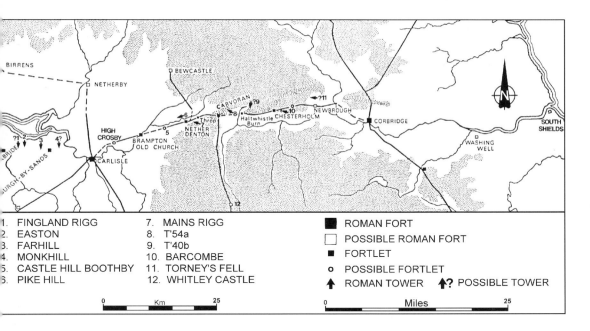

1. FINGLAND RIGG	7. MAINS RIGG	■	ROMAN FORT
2. EASTON	8. T'54a	□	POSSIBLE ROMAN FORT
3. FARHILL	9. T'40b	■	FORTLET
4. MONKHILL	10. BARCOMBE	o	POSSIBLE FORTLET
5. CASTLE HILL BOOTHBY	11. TORNEY'S FELL		
6. PIKE HILL	12. WHITLEY CASTLE	⬆ ROMAN TOWER ⬆? POSSIBLE TOWER	

9   The Stanegate system. DJW; base map reproduced by kind permission of D.J. Breeze

The Stanegate

Hadrian's Wall was far more than just a long stone wall. It was a vast and integrated defence system, which was not built completely from nothing. There had been a military presence in the area for almost 50 years by the time of Hadrian's reign and the development of the Wall can only really be understood as a progression from the so-called 'Stanegate period', during which the idea of a frontier between the Tyne and Solway evolved on the Roman road now known by its medieval name of the Stanegate (which means simply 'the stone road').

The idea that a frontier system had existed in the area before Hadrian's Wall was prompted by the existence of a number of forts, fortlets and towers which apparently predated the Wall and which lay between a few hundred metres and a mile or two to its south. Some 50 years ago only the central area was known in any detail but here, at least, a pattern seemed to emerge with a simple arrangement of alternating forts and large fortlets set out along the Roman road at about 3.5 mile intervals. Since then, however, a number of misgivings have arisen to cast doubt on whether this same pattern holds good throughout the line. Firstly, despite years of searching, only two of these fort-fortlet units have been found with certainty, with the series running (**9**): Vindolanda (fort) — Haltwhistle Burn (fortlet) — Carvoran (fort) — Throp (fortlet) — Nether Denton (fort). There is, though, strong evidence for a third fortlet at Castlehill Boothby, which would continue the sequence as far west as the fort of Old Church Brampton. To extend this system still further, however, we would need fortlets at or near High Crosby, halfway between Old Church and Carlisle, and at Grindon Hill, to the east of Vindolanda, along with a full scale fort at Newbrough further east still. But although searches have been made at all of these sites, there is still nothing known at either of the putative fortlet positions, whilst Newbrough has only produced much later fourth-century activity.

Until still more recently, the Stanegate was also only thought to run from Corbridge in the east, to Carlisle. Indeed, to the east of Corbridge, there is still a marked shortage of sites of any kind and so we cannot be sure that the system continued further. There has, however, been one major eastern discovery in recent years in the form of a fort discovered from the air at Washing Well, Whickham (**10**) on the fringes of Gateshead (McCord and Jobey 1971, 120). This site lies to the south of the Tyne, much further from the later line of the Wall than the known Stanegate sites, and begs the question of whether archaeologists have been looking in the right places, hitherto. If the Stanegate frontier did switch to the south of the river east of Corbridge, Washing Well might not stand alone. The evidence is slight, but plausible cases have been made over the years for forts (albeit of uncertain date) at Bywell (Selkirk 1983, 134ff) and Jarrow (Birley 1961, 157f), whilst at South Shields, on the coast, what may be signs of Trajanic occupation have been revealed close to the later fort and stores base (Bidwell & Speak 1994, 14ff). It remains far from proven, but it is thus not impossible that the Stanegate ran all the way to the sea.

At the other end of the line we are on much stronger ground. For, since the 1970s, our knowledge of the situation to the west of Carlisle has been greatly expanded by the discovery of a number of new sites (mostly from the air), including a coastal fort at Kirkbride on Moricambe. Many of these lie on a series of low hills, about 3km inland of the Solway, whose topographical significance is difficult to appreciate today. But in Roman times the Solway basin was an area of frequent swamps and mosses (**38**) and these otherwise undistinguished hills formed a corridor of firm ground where the military strong points lay amongst a plethora of Romano-British agricultural settlements. The road itself has also now been seen from the air here over long stretches (and occasionally excavated) and so the Stanegate certainly appears to have reached the sea in the west, even if it cannot yet be firmly proved to have straddled the entire width of the country.

The exact dating of the Stanegate system remains obscure. For the foundation dates of the installations vary considerably, from AD 71, at Carlisle, to the end of the reign of Trajan (Hadrian's predecessor) for the fortlets. It has, indeed, been suggested that the frontier might only have reached its final form in Hadrian's first years, perhaps ultimately in concert with the early stages of the Wall itself (Dobson 1986, 3ff); more recently, it has been plausibly argued that even the Stanegate road, at least on its final, superbly engineered line, might only date to the years immediately before the building of the Wall (Poulter 1998). Even so, the concept of a complex development process has been slow to gain broad recognition, despite the fact that similar sequences are well established on other frontiers (e.g. the Taunus mountain line in Germany). Recent evidence, however, now makes it clear enough that the Stanegate's development began at least in the Trajanic period (AD 96-117), and even earlier at such major sites as Corbridge, Carlisle and Vindolanda. The latter, moreover, has produced a wonderful and quite unexpected treasure in the form of an archive of writing tablets in Latin cursive script, recovered from in and around the commanding officer's residence in one of the early timber-built forts.

These offer critical evidence for the deployment of troops in the pre-mural period and one, No.22 (Bowman & Thomas 1984, 105ff), clearly demonstrates military control by an officer with the probable title *Centurio Regionarius* (Regional Centurion) based at Carlisle, as early as AD 103-5. Other documents give various insights into life on the pre-Hadrianic frontier, including unit strength reports, communications between unit commanders, logistical records and even the first known letter between women: an invitation from one fort commander's wife to the birthday party of another. The last document would suggest free travel in relatively peaceful conditions, and the emergence of evidence such as this makes it impossible to dismiss pre-Hadrianic initiatives towards frontier control.

Aerial reconnaissance is of particular help in offering insights into this evolutionary process, both for individual Stanegate sites and for the system as a whole. It tends to confirm the apparent absence over much of the line of the traditionally envisaged rigid system of alternating large and small installations, but this does not rule out the likelihood that cohesive frontier arrangements were made. There is growing evidence that many of the major installations passed through two or more developmental stages, demonstrating a far greater complexity of expansion and contraction in military deployments than had been recognised before. In particular, there are emerging signs that a number of the Stanegate forts went through a phase in which they were unusually large. Likewise, the occupation span of a number of sites has proved to be longer than had previously been supposed, and again Vindolanda is the key site for this period. The earliest fort here, of 3.5 acres, was garrisoned by the first Cohort of Tungrians at some point before AD 90, in other words more than 30 years before Hadrian's Wall was begun. In around AD 90, however, the primary western ditch was filled in to allow for an apparent doubling in the fort's size to around 7 acres (2.8 hectares). This was to accommodate the Seventh Cohort of Batavians, possibly co-brigaded with a detachment of the third Cohort of Batavians. At Vindolanda, therefore, the model for pre-Hadrianic arrangements, on current evidence, is that a normal auxiliary fort was built along the arterial road and then doubled in size to accommodate the deployment of a larger garrison. The Vindolanda evidence comes from excavation, but signs of similarly large installations have been detected from the air at other sites, such as Nether Denton (**22 & 23**), Kirkbride and Carvoran (**18**). Washing Well may show similar indications and excavations over many years at both Carlisle and Corbridge appear to show still greater complexity.

Perhaps the clearest example, however, lies on the newly discovered, so-called 'Western Stanegate' to the west of Carlisle. As has already been said, the pre-Wall frontier in this sector lay on the more elevated ground along the southern edge of the coastal mosses, well behind the coastal Wall frontier which later replaced it. One of the strategic keys to the west are the fords across the Solway estuary near the village of Burgh-by-Sands. These afforded vital crossing places to (and from) the north, which were to be used 1,200 years later by King Edward I in his Scottish campaigns. The area thus held a military value which it is difficult to appreciate when looking at the attractive but sleepy modern settlement and its surroundings, and aerial archaeology has revealed previously unsuspected signs of intense activity in the pre-Hadrianic period. In particular, no less than two new auxiliary forts have been discovered, both of which also passed through phases in which they were up to eight acres in area.

There remains the question of how these abnormally large sites fit in with the wider historical sequence prior to the construction of Hadrian's Wall. To the east at Corbridge, the Period I fort was expanded in the late 80s or early 90s, whilst at Vindolanda, as we have seen, the same process of expansion occurred around AD 90. This might suggest a close link with the redeployment of the Roman army after the abandonment of north-eastern and central Scotland. It may thus represent part of a coherent pattern that has little or nothing to do with the emergence of the smaller fortlets, which were originally thought to be such a fundamental characteristic of the Stanegate line. This new evidence therefore offers a slightly different variation on the previously held concept in which the more northerly (and also unusually large) forts at Newstead and Dalswinton were seen as the initial focus of military retrenchment. Instead, one could now argue that these northern forts were just outposts for the linear dispositions on the Stanegate and, thus, that this came to represent the northern frontier of Britain a decade or two earlier than had been thought, in the late AD 80s or early 90s.

The large expanded forts at Carlisle, Corbridge and Vindolanda can firmly account for the presence of up to 3,000 men. If the new large primary forts of Burgh-by-Sands I, Nether Denton, and possibly Carvoran, are added to this picture, on the grounds of probable contemporaneity, then the size of the garrison could be increased to up to 6,000 in the central and western sectors of the developing frontier zone. Washing Well, if it belongs to this phase, would add yet more troops and, again, there may be other sites awaiting discovery. If the strategic emphasis of the post-Agricolan arrangements, therefore, lay on the Tyne-Solway axis and not on the more forward sites, and if the bulk of the frontier's manpower was initially disposed, at least predominantly, in very large forts that may have been garrisoned by more than just a single auxiliary unit, then we would seem to have a reversion to a rather different frontier approach. During the Gask period the Romans had allowed a considerable dispersion of their frontier forces, both by employing some smaller single unit forts and by detaching small groups of men to man watchtowers and fortlets. This would have allowed detailed frontier control and surveillance, but it was most suited to relatively settled conditions in which the Romans could be confident that such dispersed groupings could operate securely, perhaps protected by intelligence cover to the north. The initial Stanegate configuration, on the other hand, may reflect a less secure, or at least less certain, situation in which it was thought to be important to maintain larger troop concentrations for immediate defence, even if this had to be done at the expense of less intensive frontier policing. Indeed, even the frontier line itself may have been somewhat diffuse at this stage, especially if it is true that the road was a relatively late addition. It should be stressed, however, that little excavation has taken place on many of the other forts mentioned here and Burgh-by-Sands I has the added complication that it overlies a pre-existing watchtower, so this model must currently remain hypothetical.

Whatever its initial configuration, the Stanegate was eventually to evolve into something more complex, which does seem to have taken a much greater interest in policing a more clear cut frontier line. Again, however, the historical context for this evolution is uncertain and there may be no direct link to any known historical event. It is tempting to wonder, however, whether it might be connected to further military retrenchment in Britain to release manpower for Trajan's Dacian and/or Parthian wars in the first two decades of the second century. At one point it was thought that evidence had been found for the destruction by hostile action at this time of the remaining Scottish Lowland forts, and thus for the Romans' expulsion from the area by force. This destruction now tends to be interpreted as organised demolition by the Romans themselves, but either way most of these sites do now seem to have gone out of use. The implied (possibly deliberate) withdrawal has always been difficult to accept in view of Trajan's militantly expansionist policies elsewhere around the Empire, but again some of the difficulties disappear if the major line held was already that on the Tyne-Solway, rather than the Scottish forts, and if that line was now merely being thickened up rather than established essentially from new.

The thickening itself took the form of a new deployment pattern which used larger numbers of more normal sized forts. Yet again, the dating is uncertain, but both pre-Wall Burgh-by-Sands forts were eventually reduced to about half their original size, as was Nether Denton and possibly others. At much the same time, at least one wholly new and more normal sized auxiliary fort was constructed at Old Church Brampton, and again there may well be others. At one point it was thought that this systematically reduced fort intervals, deliberately set at one day's march, to half a day's march but, in fact, the process was probably less neatly methodical. Nevertheless, the result was a general reduction of the system's inter-fort spacings to around seven miles which, as we have seen, was further reduced (possibly later still), at least in places, by the construction of the fortlets. These latter may be considered minor installations when compared to the forts, but they were very different sites to the tiny, *c.*24m square fortlets of the Gask frontier. The Stanegate equivalents were much larger, at close to an acre in size. Indeed, they were more akin to the large Flavian fortlet at Cargill (**colour plate 3**), at the Tay-Isla confluence (NO 163377) a little to the north-east of the Gask, and could have held far more substantial garrisons. The Stanegate fortlets also had internal buildings with stone foundations (as did some of the main buildings of the later Stanegate forts) and stone faced defensive walls and so mark a move away from the wholly turf and timber construction that had characterised the Stanegate thus far.

The system also acquired a communication system in the form of a series of towers at sites such as Pike Hill, Mains Rigg and Barcombe. Again, however, the layout of these sites cannot really be compared with the Gask towers. The latter were set out at frequent, if usually irregular, intervals and were obviously primarily designed as an observation chain. This was normal practice on most Roman frontiers, but on the Stanegate towers were far rarer. Roman towers are often referred to as 'Signal towers' almost as a generic term, whereas in fact most were really watchtowers, albeit they were given the ability to signal because there is little point in having observers unless they can tell someone what they see. On the Stanegate, however, the term may for once be quite accurate, because it is noteworthy that here the sites occur only where a signalling link between two more major installations is required.

Finally, at least parts of the Stanegate line seem eventually to have acquired the beginnings of a linear barrier defence, in this case a substantial defensive ditch. Such a feature has been seen from the air running just to the north of the road over long stretches to the west of Carlisle. Excavations by both authors have found that it was a classic V-sectioned Roman military ditch of around 2m wide and 1m or more deep, which was sometimes fronted by a timber fence or palisade. As yet, no equivalent defence has been found in the more central areas, but nor has it been looked for in a region which is anyway less productive of crop marks, and it will be interesting to see if such a feature emerges in the future.

Our knowledge of the early development of the Tyne-Solway frontier has thus advanced considerably. We can now firmly argue for a multi-phased pre-Wall development starting with Flavian occupation at a few major sites such as Carlisle, Vindolanda, and Corbridge (the latter site succeeded a campaign base just to the west at Red House). This phase was followed by a series of large, new or expanded forts, established very soon after the abandonment of most of the Scottish conquests in, or shortly after AD 87. Lastly, there was a dispersal of the garrisons into more frequent but smaller forts, with the addition of a series of fortlets and towers in the first two decades of the second century. The line may have extended from sea to sea, but certainly reached the coast in the west, and at least part of the frontier already had linear defences before Hadrian's Wall was begun.

The sites

Washing Well, NZ 219603

The important but unexcavated fort at Washing Well Whickham may prove vital to any understanding of the Stanegate frontier in the East. The fort sits on a plateau at the top of a steep stream gully, south of the River Tyne, and about three miles to the south of the line of Hadrian's Wall. Roughly one third of the multi-ditched defensive circuit, including two entrance breaks, is visible in **10** as crop marks, and more has been seen on other pictures. The site appears to show traces of two different periods. One is around 4.6 acres in area, inside the ditches, but the exact dimensions of the second, although larger, are currently unknown, whilst the order in which they were constructed will not be determined without excavation. As yet virtually nothing is known of either fort's interior. But eight very small, round crop marks (arrow 1) can be seen in the air photograph, running in from the north-east entrance of the smaller fort in two parallel lines of four. They represent the post holes for a massive timber gate structure and a similar arrangement has been seen on other air photographs at the south-east entrance (McCord and Jobey 1971, 120 & Holbrook and Speak, 1994). The terrain gives the fort a good view to the south, but no view over the Tyne valley to its north, and this has led to doubts as to whether it could be part of the frontier system. Unlike most of the forts on Hadrian's Wall, however, many of the other Stanegate sites lie in positions, such as valley bottoms, with little or no view north, so this should not be taken as conclusive. It is possible, instead, that we should be searching for an associated watchtower on the southern edge of the Tyne valley, and in visual contact with the fort to allow signalling. But even if such a tower did exist it has probably been destroyed, since much of the area is now heavily built-up.

The roughly circular enclosure visible as a crop mark in the bottom left-hand corner of the photograph is a filled in mine shaft dating to the mid- to late-seventeenth century.

10   Washing Well Whickham fort from the north-east.
Photo by kind permission of Prof. N. McCord, copyright Newcastle University

Corbridge (Latin Corstopitum*), NY 983648*

No one picture of Corbridge can do justice to one of the most complex sites in Roman Britain and one that still has much to reveal. It sat right beside the Tyne at a bridging point and was the springboard for military campaigns along Dere Street, the eastern route into Scotland. Later, it was a lynch pin of the Stanegate system, although little from these early periods now remains visible. Excavation in advance of the Hexham by-pass showed that the earliest site in the area, a supply base of substantial size, lay at Red House about a kilometre to the west. By the end of the first century AD, however, the focus had moved to the main Corbridge site at the crossroads between Dere Street and the Stanegate, where it remained for the rest of the Roman period. Here, a complex succession of forts developed, reflecting the ebb and flow of events along the northern frontier, before the site changed nature to become a largely civilian town, albeit one which retained a military presence.

The preserved remains visible today belong largely to the late second and early third centuries and represent only a small part of the total area of the site, more of which is occasionally visible from the air. The air photograph (**colour plate 4**) shows the Stanegate road itself (1) forming one of the main streets of the later town and with a number of major buildings fronting onto it. To the left of the road lie two early third-century walled compounds, separated by a side street (2 & 3), in which detachments of

11   Corbridge, showing Dere Street as a scorch mark. DJW

the sixth and twentieth legions were based. The parent legions occupied fortresses at York and Chester respectively and these are so far the only legionary troops known to have been stationed in the immediate Wall area. On the opposite side of the Stanegate, in front of the modern museum and car park (7), lie two unusually large military style granaries (4). These replaced a more normally sized pair retained from an earlier mid-secondary fort, the last of no less than four forts to be built on the site. These buildings are in an exceptional state of preservation and alongside the nearer of the two can be seen the line of an almost equally well-preserved aqueduct (5). This brought water into the town and ends in a fountain and large stone tank beside the road. Closest to the camera, the remains of a vast courtyard building (6) of the 170s can be seen. The latter seems never to have been finished, and it had probably all but vanished when the legionary compounds were built. But it was obviously intended to be a structure of unusual grandeur, for the masonry involved is of a dramatically superior quality to anything else within the excavated area. It is often described as a store building, but its elegant construction would seem unnecessary for such a utilitarian role and it may have been intended as a market place (*forum*) or some other public building. Whatever the case, it overlay the rest of the central range of the same fort that the granaries originally derived from and the remains of the former *praetorium* (see appendix) can be seen clearly within the courtyard, with less distinct signs of the *principia* beyond them. A number of other smaller buildings on both sides of the road appear to be temples.

Just outside the modern display area, the Stanegate makes a near right-angled junction with Dere Street, which can occasionally be seen via scorch marks from the air (**11**, arrowed). Major crossroads often formed the nuclei around which Roman towns formed and Corbridge was no exception. For this area is the centre of town and excavations at the start of the twentieth century found other important structures, such as baths, beside the aqueduct a little further to the north.

Although Corbridge has long been the scene of major excavations, the complexity of the site has still been unravelled in part through many years of air photography (Bishop & Dore 1988, 8ff). Beneath the stone buildings amongst which the visitor walks today lie the remains of four earlier, largely timber, periods. The discovery from the air of a line of northern defences, along with its north-east and north-west corners, showed that these underlying structures belonged, as mentioned, to a series of earlier auxiliary forts. Composite air photography across many seasons thus allowed archaeologists to demonstrate the overall context for the early periods they had excavated further south in the town centre. These were eventually shown to have involved a primary fort that was later replaced by a second installation, which itself yielded three separate phases of development in its internal buildings. Furthermore, it was possible to show that some of the roads of the later town reflected military predecessors.

Air photography has also produced further information about the second-century and later civil settlement, particularly where it lies along the Stanegate itself. For traces of extensive civilian activity can be seen all round the excavated area in suitable crop conditions. To the east and west, on both sides of the Roman road, strip buildings have been identified, demonstrating that the town was at least 500 metres across. Behind the two legionary compounds other buildings were revealed towards the Tyne whilst, to the north-east, in the angle of Corchester Lane, a series of pits may represent traces of quarrying and/or an area of rubbish disposal. Further to the east, on the edge of the modern town of Corbridge, the eastern side of a large, as yet unidentified, enclosure has also been observed. Air photography is thus continuing to provide information about the site and its size at its maximum extent, as well as setting past and future excavations into their wider context.

Newbrough

To the west of Corbridge, the course of the Stanegate road is uncertain for several miles until just beyond its crossing of the North Tyne (*c*.NY 909685). From here it runs through Fourstones to the village of Newbrough, where a modern B-road joins it and follows its course for most of the way to Vindolanda. Archaeologists have long expected to find a Stanegate period fort in or around this village, mainly on spacing grounds. But, until recently, the only site that had been found was a fourth-century fortlet of about three quarters of an acre (Birley 1961, 147f) under Newbrough churchyard (NY 868680). This was obviously far too late to belong to the Stanegate and, although there have been only very limited excavations on the site, there were no indications that the fortlet might overlie an earlier installation. Recent air photography, however, has found another possible candidate site, about 1km to the east, at Sitgate Lane, on the opposite side of the village (NY 877677). This is a *c*.six acre ditched enclosure of obvious Roman military type (**12**, arrow 1 & **13**). But unfortunately, despite a series of fairly clear pictures which, between them, now show almost the entire ditch circuit (except for the north-western corner, which has been built over), we also have doubts as to whether this site represents the missing fort. It is certainly possible, and only excavation will settle the matter for certain, but the ditch appears rather narrow for a permanent fort, and it seems more likely to be a Roman temporary camp.

Inside the six acre enclosure air photography also reveals a much smaller (*c*.0.75 acre) double ditched enclosure (**12**, arrow 2 & **13**), and initially it seemed possible that this might represent another fortlet. As the site has emerged more clearly, however, it has begun to look rather less regular than one would expect of a Roman military site. This is not conclusive for, as we shall see, the known Stanegate fortlet of Haltwhistle Burn has a distinctly irregular ditch system, and again only excavation can settle the matter. But for the moment, the site appears more likely to have a native origin.

Newbrough sits at the bottom of a fairly steep valley, close to the River Tyne and if there was a Stanegate installation on the site it would have had an urgent need for satellite signal/watchtowers to provide longer range observation cover and communications. None have yet been found in the area, but one ideal site would have been Warden Hill, a pronounced peak about two miles to the east of the village which is also the site of an Iron Age hillfort (NY 904678). The prehistoric site appears from the air to have a number of later structures built into it (**colour plate 5**) and these might well repay further investigation.

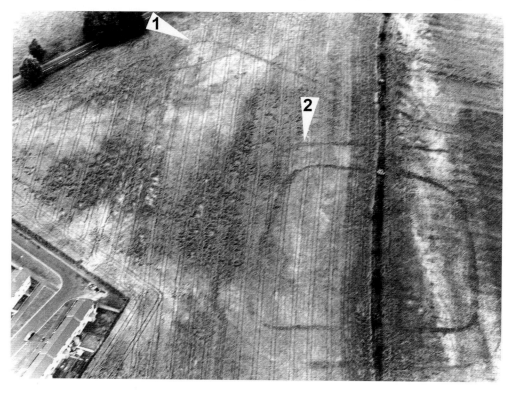

12   Newbrough Sitgate from the south-west

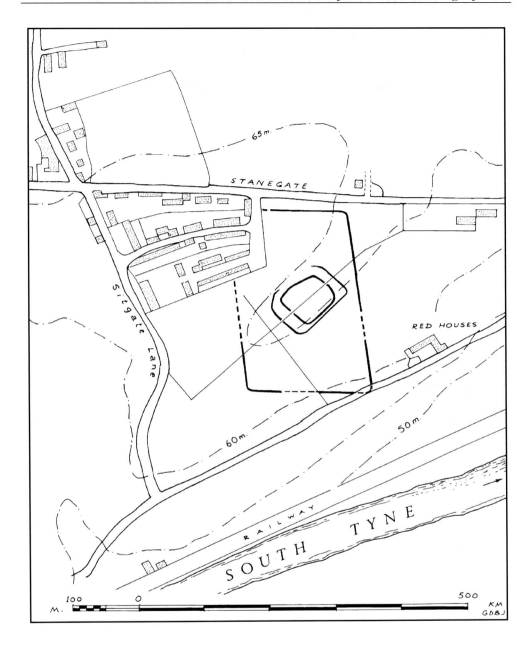

13   *Newbrough Sitgate: plan*

Chesterholm (Latin, Vindolanda), NY 771664

Although it lies some distance behind Hadrian's Wall, the Roman fort at Chesterholm is deservedly one of the best known forts in the frontier area, thanks to the ongoing excavations of the Vindolanda Trust. It is also possibly the only Roman fort in Britain that has come to be better known by its Latin name than its modern equivalent. The site began as early as the AD 80s and was, as we have seen, a major site on the Stanegate frontier, although the visible remains seen in **colour plate 6** belong to a later period. The Stanegate road itself runs across the background of the photograph (arrow 1), here still in use as a farm road. In the foreground the playing card shaped outline of the late fort is crisply preserved and the third- and fourth-century headquarters building (arrow 2) and commanding officer's house (arrow 3) have been conserved for display. This fort, however, at around 3.5 acres, is less than half the size of largest of the pre-Wall forts, which extended over the whole of the area to the left of the visible fort, which is now covered by the remains of a later civilian town, or *vicus*. The only surviving sign of its presence lies in the fact that the *vicus'* main street is set at a noticeable angle to the visible fort's own *Via principalis* (see appendix). This is because the township followed the street pattern of the larger fort, which was built on a different alignment to its successor.

The air photograph also shows a number of unusual circular structures underlying and so predating the late fort (**colour plate 6,** 4), which now appear to extend over an area larger than the fort itself. These are reminiscent of native round houses but are stone built, something which is usually associated with Roman construction methods. There has been speculation that they represent a time during which the site may have been used to house native prisoners or hostages taken during a campaign. Hostage taking to ensure the good behaviour of tribal rulers was certainly a standard Roman practice and this is a perfectly plausible interpretation. But it is doubtful whether it can ever be proved (or disproved) unless we are lucky enough to find relevant epigraphic evidence. This may not be as hopeless a quest as it might sound, however. Excavation beneath the late *vicus* has demonstrated the existence of archaeological layers dating back to the first century, and rich organic deposits have been located here in waterlogged levels now known to form part of a sequence of turf and timber forts of approximately AD 90-125. This area yielded remarkable finds of well-preserved pollen and insect remains, together with timber, textiles, leather and even straw floor coverings. Amongst these outstanding remains, the excavators found quantities of wafer-thin sheets of wood and recognised them as representing writing tablets covered with Latin script. The texts are often visible on recovery, but require immediate conservation if their contents are to be painstakingly deciphered. The mass of material recovered in this way — well over 1,000 fragments to date (Bowman and Thomas 1984 & 1994) — forms the most important discovery of its kind, because it derives from a clearly defined archaeological context. Some of the tablets were found in what must have been the commanding officer's house (which, they tell us, he shared with his wife). Others have been recovered from the rear of the early fort's southern rampart, where they were apparently swept to be destroyed on a bonfire. Amongst a wealth of other information, they make Vindolanda one of the few sites for which the Stanegate period garrison is known: the first cohort of Tungrians and the ninth cohort of Batavians (the latter from the Rhine delta), whilst we know from inscriptions that the Wall period garrisons were the third cohort of Nervians, followed by the fourth cohort of Gauls.

Outside the visible fort a variety of structures can be seen. Towards the bottom of the picture (arrow 5) an early bath building has recently been found, which may be associated with the Stanegate period forts. The baths for the later fort have long been known and were situated further to the north-west, in the *vicus* (arrow 9). To the left of the early baths, a rectangular walled area can be seen (arrow 6). This is a modern reconstruction of part of Hadrian's Wall, in both its turf and stone incarnations (see below), and was designed partly to provide an idea of how the Wall would have looked when first built, but also as an experiment to see how durable it would have been and how much maintenance it might have needed.

Further to the north, as already mentioned, the photograph shows how the road leading from the west (left) gate of the fort was flanked by a series of stone buildings belonging to the civilian *vicus*. These are mostly long narrow structures, known as strip buildings, which served as shops, houses and workshops (and possibly all three at once), but amongst them are a number of more notable structures. Towards the left-hand side of the picture a series of water tanks is visible (7) which were fed by an aqueduct that entered the site from the north. The square of foundations towards the top left-hand corner of the picture (8) is a newly discovered temple, that was actually under excavation at the time the air photograph was taken (spring 2001), whilst the large courtyard building (arrow 10) at the western fringe of the built-up area (as currently excavated) may be the remains of a *mansio*: a state run inn for official travelers.

Vindolanda sits in something of a basin with higher ground to its east and west and only a limited view north. It thus relied for communications and observation cover on a satellite watchtower, which during the Stanegate period was located just over 1km to the north-east, near the summit of Barcombe Hill (NY 783668). Figure **14** shows the round

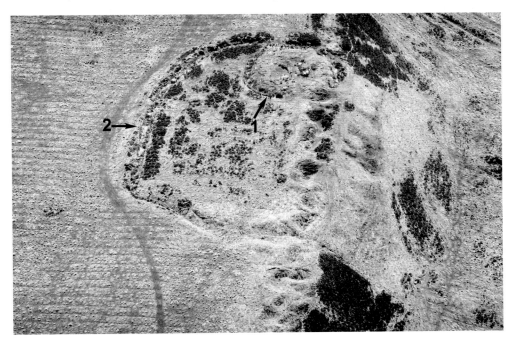

14   Barcombe Watchtower and hillfort from the north-east. DJW

45

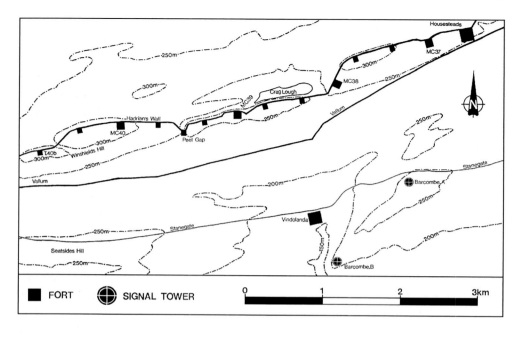

15   Map of the environs of Vindolanda, showing both Barcombe watchtowers. DJW

ditch of the Roman tower (arrow 1) set inside the larger enclosure of an earlier Iron Age hillfort (arrow 2), with a steep drop to the north (right). The site has superb long-range views in every direction except the south (where the fort itself has a reasonable view) and was an ideal signalling and lookout position. It has been excavated twice. Sadly the first dig, by W. Aitchison, was never published and no records appear to survive. But a note by E. Birley (1961, 147) reported a timber tower being found in the interior, similar to those on the Gask frontier. A later excavation by P. Woodfield (1988) failed to find this structure, perhaps because the earlier work had destroyed it, but was able to supply dating evidence. The result was rather surprising. Unlike many of the Stanegate sites, which were abandoned shortly after the construction of Hadrian's Wall, Vindolanda remained in use throughout the rest of the Roman occupation and would have continued to need a relay site for its signals. Yet the tower seems to have gone out of use fairly early in the second century. At one time this was something of a puzzle, since the site seemed so vital to the fort's operations and security. But it was solved some years ago when a second, slightly later, stone built tower was found on the western flank of Barcombe (**15**, Barcombe, B), a little to the south-east of Vindolanda (Woolliscroft, Swain and Lockett 1992). This new site does not show well from the air, although it can still be seen from the fort itself as a slight hump on the southern skyline. Its position, though, made it eminently suited to continue the signalling role (Woolliscroft 2001) and, unlike its predecessor, it did have an impressive view to the south.

Haltwhistle Burn Fortlet, NY 715662

Three and a half miles to the west of Vindolanda lie the well-preserved remains of the Stanegate fortlet of Haltwhistle Burn (**16**, 1). The site measures just under an acre in area and sits on Haltwhistle Common, just to the east of a steep ravine carved by the burn after which the fortlet is named. Immediately to its south, the Stanegate road (arrow 3) shows clearly on the air photograph, running on an embankment towards its crossing of the burn, which lies just out of shot, beyond the bottom left-hand corner of the picture (*see* **56**).

Excavations by Gibson and Simpson in 1908 (**17**) revealed the presence of three (rather than the normal four) single portal gates, two of which were set in slight in-turns of the fortlet's rampart which, itself, had a stone outer facing. The internal structures were also of stone and were set out in a somewhat irregular manner around a skeletal internal road system. They included a small granary (**17**, IV) and what might be a barrack with a separate centurion's block (**17**, II and III). The pottery recovered appears to belong to the period of the Emperor Trajan or the very early years of Hadrian, presumably just before the construction of the Wall. Seen from the air, however, one of the most striking features of the site is the irregular and apparently oversized nature of the defensive ditch circuit (**16**, arrow 2), within which the far more regular fortlet sits. This apparent mismatch might suggest that the ditch was originally dug to accompany a slightly larger, but less regular, installation earlier in the Stanegate period. No sign of such an installation was detected during the 1908 excavations, and no further work has been carried out on the site since. But, as this predecessor would probably have been of turf and timber construction, the traces might easily have been missed and it would be interesting to see what excavations on the present berm would reveal, particularly outside the fortlet's northern side or south-western corner, where the rampart can be anything up to 27 metres from the ditch.

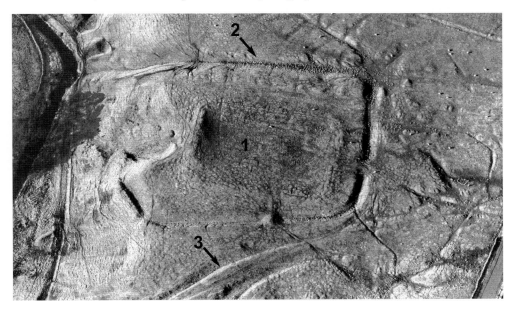

16   Haltwhistle Burn fortlet from the south-east

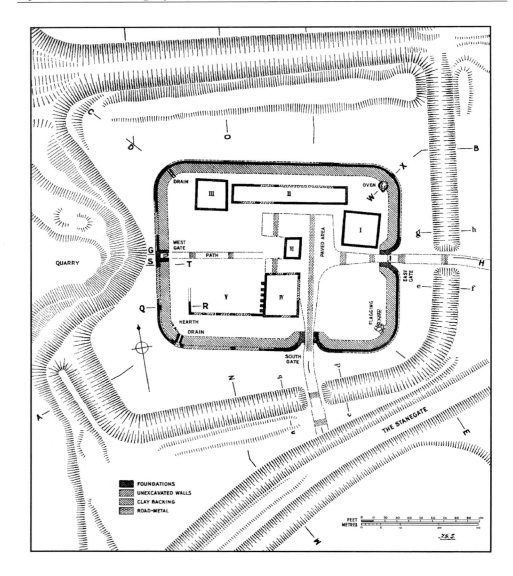

17   *Haltwhistle Burn fortlet excavation plan*

Carvoran Fort (Latin Magna), NY 666656

From Corbridge westwards, the Stanegate has been running along the northern side of the
South Tyne valley, getting slowly further from the river. Three and a quarter miles to the
west of Haltwhistle Burn however it encounters another major landscape feature in the
Thirwall Gap, a natural north-south route through the line. To secure this strategic point
a fort was established astride the crest of a hill at Carvoran (above and just to the east of
the modern village of Greenhead), from where it could command extensive views. This
is also the point at which the Stanegate meets another major Roman road, the Maiden

Way, which leads away to the south, past the hinterland fort of Whitley Castle, to reach the Roman road across Stainmore (the modern A66) at the fort of Kirkby Thore.

The fort lies just beside the modern Carvoran Roman army museum, but has been relatively little excavated. The northern rampart is fairly prominent (**colour plate 7**, arrow 1) and an angle tower is displayed in the north-west corner (arrow 2), yet although the whole of the rest of the defensive circuit can just be made out in the air photograph, it is actually easier to trace on the ground and no internal detail can be seen. The visible fort may not have been the first on the site, however. Like Vindolanda, Carvoran was retained in use after the construction of Hadrian's Wall as one of the chain of Wall forts. But because of the importance of its position it is almost certainly much earlier in origin and it always continued to lie a little behind both the Wall itself (**18 & 19**) and its huge rearward ditch and rampart defence known as the Vallum (see below). The full situation remains uncertain because of the lack of excavation, but there is a possibility that, like Vindolanda, the site was once much larger — or was intended to be so. There are a number of possible strands of evidence. Firstly, the site's Roman name was *Magna*, which means 'big' or 'great', hardly a fitting description for the rather small fort visible today. Secondly, the Vallum makes a clear deviation to the north of the fort as if to avoid something that was already there when it was built. It would have missed the visible fort by a comfortable margin even if it had continued on straight, so something, presumably much larger, must have been there, possibly an earlier fort. The only alternative explanation offered to date is that the Vallum was deviating

18   *Carvoran possible early phase, from the north-west*

to avoid a patch of marshy ground, but this has never seemed wholly plausible, especially as its own massive ditch would have radically improved the area's drainage. Until recently, however, there was no direct evidence for such a fort, but the air photograph (**18**) may have changed matters somewhat.

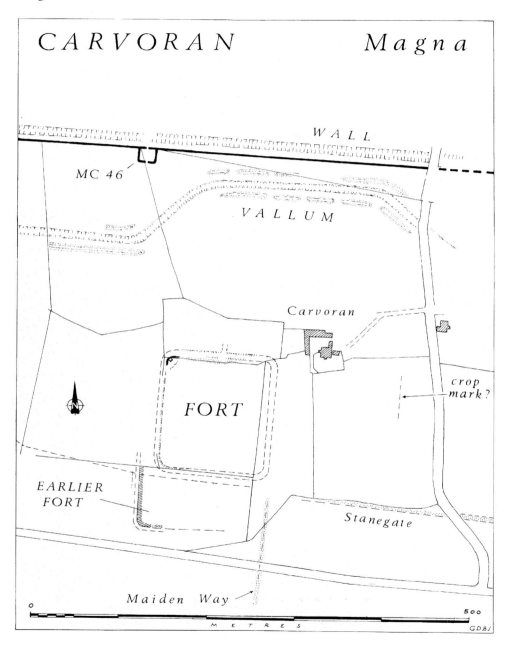

19 *Carvoran, plan of the possible air photographic features*

This photograph was taken from a significantly higher altitude than **colour plate 7** and the image quality is less than perfect. Nevertheless the picture could prove to be important because, as well as the line of Hadrian's Wall (arrow 5), the Vallum deviation (arrow 4) and the faint remains of Wall milecastle 46 (arrow 6), it shows what appears to be the rounded corner of a Roman military-style ditch (arrow 2) a little to the south-west

20   *The Thirwall Gap from the south, with Glenwhelt Leazes temporary camp*

of the visible fort (1). There is also a very faint north-south running mark to the east of the visible fort, which could be another ditch (arrow 3). When superimposed on a plan of the site (**19**), these two marks seem as though they may be part of the same ditch circuit and, if so, they line up rather neatly with the Vallum deviation, which might well, therefore, have been avoiding the northern side of the same enclosure. This would suggest an early fort of at least twice the size of the visible site, if not larger. For the moment, however, it should be stressed that we have no direct evidence for the north-south dimensions of this putative large fort. Moreover, the existence of the north-south running ditch has recently been called into at least some doubt by a large scale geophysical study of the area, which proved unable to trace the feature (although it did reveal *vicus* structures around the known fort). There is some slight evidence for early occupation, in the form of a grain measure which had been stamped with the name of the Emperor Domitian (ruled AD 81-96), but it is possible that this had been in use for many years when it was discarded. Until more work can be done on this site, therefore, preferably including excavations on the possible south-west corner, the case for a large early fort, whilst suggestive, cannot be regarded as proven.

No evidence has yet been recovered to tell us the garrison of the putative Stanegate fort, but by the mid-second century, the Wall fort was occupied by *Coh I Hamiorum Sagittaria*, a 500-strong unit of Syrian archers. In the mid-second century, this same unit was to occupy the fort of Bar Hill on the Antonine Wall in Scotland which, interestingly, was also set back slightly from the line. By the fourth century, however, the garrison had changed to the second cohort of Dalmatians, another 500-strong unit, this time of infantry from the area of modern Yugoslavia.

To the west of the fort the ground slopes down steeply into the Thirwall Gap, over which the fort itself has a spectacular view. Something of the strategic significance of this pass can be seen in **20**. For it now carries a modern road and the Carlisle to Newcastle railway, both of which use it to cross from the Tyne to the Irthing valleys using manageable gradients. In Roman times the Stanegate and the Wall each crossed the pass at right angles, the latter blocking it completely, and both lines are visible on the air photograph. The Stanegate can be seen climbing the steep western side of the pass on a north-westerly course, on a terrace cut into the valley side (arrow 1). It then turns sharply to the left and heads away to the west (arrow 2). About 100m further away (north), Hadrian's Wall's Vallum can be traced (arrow 3), whilst the Wall itself passes under the farm buildings beyond. In the foreground, the playing card shape of the three acre temporary camp of Glenwhelt Leazes is clearly visible (arrow 4), but Carvoran itself is out of shot to the right, as is its medieval counterpart, Thirwall Castle.

Throp Fortlet, NY 632659

Two and a quarter miles west of Carvoran, the Stanegate reaches the 0.9 acre fortlet of Throp. The installation sits just north of the Roman road, on a small rise with an excellent field of view, and was excavated by Simpson (1913) shortly before the First World War. As can be seen in **21** (arrowed), the site is much less well preserved than Haltwhistle Burn, but the air photograph, taken in very low light, does bring out the entire circuit of the defences. Part of the reason for its poorer preservation is, no doubt, the richer land on which it stands, which has long been subject to ploughing. But the fortlet also lacked the stone-faced defensive wall found at Haltwhistle Burn, and instead had a turf rampart, albeit founded on a stone base. Throp has a ditch which does seem to have been designed to fit it, rather than a larger installation, and is in fact slightly larger and squarer than Haltwhistle Burn. But the defences of the two sites are otherwise broadly comparable. Throp has a similarly unusual entrance layout, with only two, rather than the normal four, gates, and these are again single portal affairs which, like Haltwhistle Burn, are set in the east and south sides. Here, however, the gates are set flush with the rampart line, rather than being placed in reentrants, and both yielded six post holes (arranged in a dice six formation) which were presumably designed to carry gate towers.

Sadly, the internal buildings are an almost complete mystery. There were no signs of the stone structures found at Haltwhistle Burn, even as trenches left by stone robbers, and so they may have been made of timber. This is not absolutely certain, since Simpson reports that stone was once regularly ploughed up on the site. But, whatever the case, by the time of the excavation, many years of cultivation had removed any evidence, apart from a few small expanses of flagging, and an oven built into the rampart back. A small quantity of dating evidence was recovered, however, which suggested that the site was more or less contemporary with Haltwhistle Burn, but although it too went out of use once Hadrian's Wall was built, there were signs that it may have had a second occupation much later, in the fourth century. If so, this might be related to the fourth-century fortlet at Newbrough and it is tempting to speculate once again whether this site might also have had an early second-century phase. That said, there were no structural signs of the sort we might expect in support of the finds evidence, for example a refurbishment of the defences, and so this later usage might have been casual.

21 Throp fortlet from the south-east

Nether Denton Fort, NY 596646

Nether Denton lies in the Irthing valley on a bluff overlooking the river, just under two and a quarter miles to the west of Throp, and partly overlain by a church and two houses. Nothing is visible on the surface and until recently it was one of the least understood of the Stanegate forts. Indeed, for many years, its very existence was only known from occasional finds on the site, notably a quantity of Roman coins and pottery (of the 80s to the early second century) found during the building of a rectory in 1868. Trial excavations in 1933, by Simpson and St Joseph (1934), revealed traces of structures inside an east-west running turf rampart to the south of the church, but the details were sketchy and no plan was published. Simpson was later buried here and clay and cobble foundations were uncovered during the digging of his grave (Birley 1961, 142).

This data, combined with the general topography of the site, suggested a fort of around three acres, but air photography in the famous drought year of 1976 revolutionised the situation by showing that the known fort, like those at other Stanegate sites, was in fact the successor to another much larger fort, of *c*.8.1 acres. Indeed, there may even have been two earlier forts on the site. Figure **22** shows the southern and western ditches of the large site revealed as crop marks, with the south-western corner particularly clear. There are, though, two sets of ditches and the outer ditch (arrow 1) is much further from the inner (arrow 2) than one would normally expect in an installation that simply had a double ditched defense. It is possible, therefore, that a large fort was replaced at some point by a slightly smaller one, which was itself later reduced to about half its original north-south length by inserting the east-west running defences found in 1933, whose line appears as a faint mark in the field in front of the churchyard (arrow 3 and **23**).

22   *Nether Denton fort from the south-east*

Alternatively, and only more excavation can address this issue with certainty, the arrow 2 ditch could belong to an annex of the known three acre fort. Annexes are a regular feature of Roman forts, especially those built of turf and timber, but they are currently somewhat understudied, which means that their function is less than certain. They may have housed and protected some civilian activity and they may have acted as secure compounds to protect military property, such as vehicles, for which there was not enough room in the fort. They also often held buildings such as bath blocks and workshops whose activities might have posed too great a fire risk to be sited inside the fort.

In addition to the information on the fort itself, the 1976 photographs also revealed signs of activity to its west. Figure **24** shows the south-west corner of the large fort already seen (arrow 1), but it also shows a dark band crossing the ditch, which may be a later road. In the next field to the west (left) another track can be seen (arrow 2) curving towards the top right-hand corner of the picture, whilst the Stanegate itself runs across the southern end of the field (arrow 3) just north of the modern road (which otherwise overlies it through much of this area). In between this lattice of tracks, the crop marks of a number of pits and linear features can be seen, which may represent the buildings or property boundaries of a *vicus* around the fort. Again, this needs to be tested by excavation but if so it cannot be the full extent of the site. Artefacts and traces of buildings were also found in

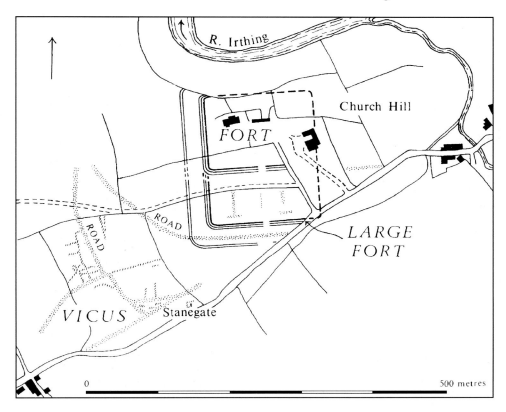

23   *Plan of the aerial evidence for Nether Denton fort and vicus*

24   *Nether Denton fort vicus from the south-east*

the field across the modern road to the south of the fort in 1933. Indeed, the town may have been substantial, for there have been finds of cremation urns over the years, from an area about 700m to the west of the fort (Welfare 1974), which suggests that a cemetery was once located there, and these were often sited on the fringes of settlements.

Nether Denton's valley bottom location does not provide it with very good views and, in particular, it is not intervisible with Throp. To allow signal communications, therefore, what is almost certainly a signal tower at Mains Rigg (NY 613652) may have been constructed at this period, although as yet there is no firm dating evidence. The site is clearly visible from the air as a roughly square ditch circuit (**25**, arrowed) on a hill side just above a modern level crossing and it has both Nether Denton and Throp in view. No internal detail is now visible, but excavations in 1928 (Richmond 1929, 314f) and 1971 (unpublished) revealed the base of a stone tower roughly 21ft square. This had no entrance at ground floor level, presumably as a security precaution, so that access could only be gained by means of a (possibly retractable) ladder to an upper floor.

Nether Denton also had another stone tower to its north-west at Pike Hill, which was later incorporated into the line of Hadrian's Wall. This site lay on much higher ground and would have greatly enhanced the fort's observation cover and its communications towards the west. It was largely destroyed by nineteenth-century road building and is not particularly visible from the air, but a small part of its masonry (which includes a ground floor entrance) can still be seen at NY 577647.

25   *Mains Rigg tower from the south-east*

Castle Hill Boothby fortlet, NY 545630

In the early 1930s, whilst searching for the next Stanegate site west of Nether Denton, F.G. Simpson's attention was drawn to a field just over three miles to the west of the fort which sat on a bluff overlooking the Irthing and which, for no visible reason, was called Castle Hill. In 1933 he conducted trenching on the site and, although no plan was ever published, a substantial ditch and clay rampart were discovered, in association with Roman pottery of a similar date to that found at Haltwhistle Burn and Throp. Simpson (1934) thus suggested that he had found another fortlet of the same type. Since that time no further work has been done on the site and there has been a tendency to ignore or even cast doubt on its existence. The field is also generally in pasture and tends not to produce crop marks. There is, however, one remarkable air photograph of the site, taken by the late Prof. J.K. St Joseph, which deserves to be much better known. The picture (**26**) shows two sides of a small playing card shaped ditched enclosure (arrow 1) as a crop mark. The site sits perched above the southern side of the Irthing Valley, with its northern end badly eroded. But there are signs of an entrance break in its eastern (long axis) ditch just before the field wall at the bluff edge. Interestingly, there is no sign of a break in the short axis southern ditch, and this would fit perfectly with what we have already seen at Haltwhistle Burn and Throp where only two full sized gates were present, one of which was located towards one end of one of the long axis sides, and the other in the middle of the short axis side to its right. If this is a fortlet, we would, therefore, expect the other gate to have been in the now vanished northern side. That said, the photograph also shows a very straight

26   Castle Hill Boothby fortlet from the north-east. © Crown Copyright/MOD

linear feature to the south of the site (arrow 2) which might be the Stanegate road (whose course is largely unknown in this sector); if so, it would be odd for a fortlet not to have an entrance oriented towards it. Nevertheless, the picture is certainly enough to prove the existence of a substantial defended enclosure which is consistent with a fortlet, on a site which has already yielded Roman dating evidence, and more excavation is now urgently needed to settle its identity for certain.

Old Church Brampton fort, NY 510615

Two and a half miles to the west of Castle Hill, the 3.7 acre fort of Old Church Brampton stands at the top of a prominent scarp, above and immediately to the south of the River Irthing. The site is rarely responsive to air photography, but much of what can be seen is shown in **colour plate 8**. The Stanegate road itself ran slightly to the north of the fort and can still be seen today (here in deep shadow) as a farm track running down to the river. The course of the road is otherwise poorly understood to the west of Nether Denton and this is one of the few visible stretches.

The church of Old St Martin's, visible towards the left-hand side of the photograph (arrow 1), is situated in the north-east corner of the fort, of which about a third lies in its graveyard and two thirds in the field behind. The south and west ramparts are marked by earth banks, now topped by a line of trees (arrow 2), and both can be seen from the air along with the typical curving south-west corner. Limited excavations in 1935 (Simpson & Richmond 1936) established the presence of the timber buildings of

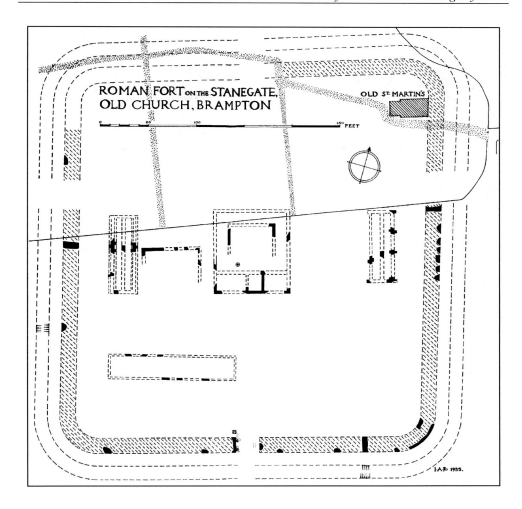

27 *Old Church Brampton fort, excavation plan*

the central range (**27**) and demonstrated that the fort faced towards the north. Two granaries were identified at opposite ends of the *Via Principalis*, with a headquarters building in the normal central position alongside a fourth building, which may be the commanding officer's house. A single barrack block was also identified in the retentura to the south. Only limited dating evidence was recovered, but the site seems to have had a similar occupation history to Haltwhistle Burn and Throp. The fort might thus have been built relatively late in the Stanegate sequence and certainly after the beginning of the second century. Unlike Vindolanda, Carvoran and Nether Denton, neither the excavations nor air photography have shown any sign of a larger fort preceding the 3.7-acre site, either underneath it or in the vicinity, and this would support the case for the fort being a late addition to the line.

28   *Carlisle, the area of the Roman fort and town, from the north-west*

Carlisle (Latin, Luguvalium), NY 399559

Although little can now been seen, either on the ground or from the air, Carlisle is one of the most important archaeological complexes in the frontier area, and one that reflects the history of both military and civilian activity near the tidal limit of the River Eden. Much excavation has taken place since the 1970s and the results give new perspectives to our understanding of the development of the Roman presence.

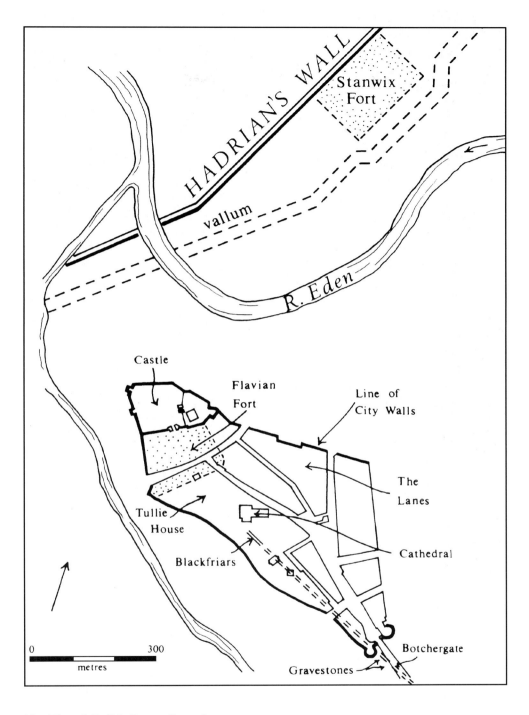

29   *Plan of Carlisle Roman fort and town*

It was long ago established that remarkably well-preserved timber work lay below parts of the area between the cathedral and the castle. Moreover, the latter (as shown in **28**) stands on the tip of a ridge overlooking the Eden, in a position with obvious defensive potential. Recent excavations next to Tullie House Museum and to the south of the castle by the City of Carlisle Archaeological Unit have made sense of the puzzle by locating the south gate and adjacent interior of a remarkably well-preserved turf and timber Roman fort. The date of its foundation is now known from dendrochronology to lie in the early AD 70s, almost certainly in late 71, and the establishment of the fort is thus presumably linked to the Flavian advance into northern England (and just possibly Scotland) under the governor Petillius Cerialis, long before Hadrian's Wall had even been conceived.

With the coming of the Wall, Carlisle continued in use but the military focus switched across the river to the present suburb of Stanwix, where a new fort (**29**) was set on a ridge north of the River Eden, some 1,200m to the north-east of the castle. Nevertheless, the importance of Carlisle as a focal point was reflected in continued development on the south side of the river. The area of the early timber fort was retained under military control with varying degrees of intensity until the later second century, but by then Carlisle was on the way to becoming a substantial civilian centre, as the capital of the north-western tribe known as the Carvetii. This was one of only two points on the frontier where there were moves towards the development of major civilian towns, rather than the village-sized *vici* which developed around most of the forts elsewhere on the line. At Corbridge, as we have seen, the civilian settlement, built over the remains of successive forts, contained two small walled legionary compounds set right in the town centre. But, so far as we are aware, no enclosing defensive wall was ever constructed around the settlement as a whole. The emergence of Carlisle as a cantonal capital, on the other hand, may have raised it to a superior status. The settlement developed substantial stone defences (**29**), which enclosed most of the hilltop to the south-east of the castle and eventually formed the basis of the medieval city's defences.

Like Vindolanda, Carlisle has begun to produce writing tablets and, amongst other information, these have now given us the name of one of its early garrisons, probably in the AD 80s: a Gallic cavalry unit called *Ala Gallorum Sebosiana*.

Burgh-by-Sands, NY 3258

The next key site on the Stanegate lies some four miles to the north-west of Carlisle at Burgh-by-Sands, where a group of sites is now known in and around the modern village. The area's present tranquillity belies its earlier tactical importance for, as already mentioned, it lies on the south side of the lowest Solway fords, the Sandwath (Durnock Wath) and the Peat Wath. These once made it a major crossing point, as witnessed by Edward I's death here whilst preparing to cross the fords with an army during his final campaign against Robert the Bruce. In the Roman period, a second- to fourth-century fort (Burgh II) lay where the eastern end of the village now stands. But two other forts have been revealed by aerial photography, each of which shows a number of stages of development (**32**).

30   Burgh-by-Sands fort I from the south

Fort I, NY 325582 (South Fort) occupies a hilltop on the line of the Burgh to Moorhouse road, some 1,000 yards south of the village centre. A combination of both aerial photography and excavation here have produced the following sequence:

Phase 1   Before the building of the fort, a Gask style circular watch-post, *c*.20m in diameter, was constructed close to the highest point of the hill (**colour plate 9**, arrow 2). This consisted of a 2.3m wide ring ditch, 1.8m deep and backed by a 4-4.5m wide rampart, revetted with timber at its front. A single entranceway lay on the north-east side of the enclosure and a timber watchtower lay within the bank itself, built on four main uprights, each *c*.25cm square.

Phase 2   The site of the watchtower was subsequently levelled and overlain by a two-period fort. The first enclosed approximately 7 acres and extended either side of the modern minor road (**30**, arrows 1 & 2, plus **colour plate 9**, arrow 1). It thus straddled a ridge running south from Burgh-by-Sands village. The northern defences of the large fort were sectioned at two points after the entire defensive circuit was revealed from the air in the drought of 1984. A small trial trench revealed the presence of timber buildings in the interior.

Phase 3   The site was reduced in size to *c*.3.7 acres by constructing a new eastern ditch and rampart that partly overlay the eastern edge of the initial watchtower (**30 & colour plate 9**, arrow 3). As a result, the fort now lay wholly to the west of the modern road, occupying the crest of the ridge. Two entrances are visible in the air photographs: one about halfway along the southern side (**colour plate 9**) and the other a third of the way south along the eastern reducing defences, near the fork visible in the modern road. The interior again contained timber buildings, but air photographs also show clear traces of a stone-built *principia* and granary (**colour plate 9**, arrows 4 & 5), which, although unexcavated, seem to come from a main range which fits wholly within the reduced fort, and so presumably belong to this phase. This is confirmed by the fact that both the gate layout and the *principia* show that the fort was oriented to the north (see appendix), whilst the large, phase 2, fort must have faced either to the east or, more probably, to the west. For forts almost always face along, and not at right angles to, their long axes. Trenching has shown that the new eastern rampart was *c.*6.5m across with a carefully laid foundation of large pebbles, above which the clay core of the rampart itself had been braced with timber uprights. The pottery from the site cannot be dated more accurately than that it lies within the period AD 90 to 130. This means that the watchtower and both phases of the fort appear to have been occupied within a relatively brief span at, or more probably before, the beginning of the Wall period.

Fort III, NY 316587 (the West End Fort), was first seen from the air in 1977 and seems to have followed a similar pattern of reduction to fort I. An apparently secondary ditch and rampart (**31**, arrow 2) cut off the southernmost 290m of the interior to pare an even larger 8.4 acre site (arrow 1) down to 5.13 acres. The presence of this third fort, so close to those already known in the area, came as a complete surprise, so much so that it was initially assumed to be a temporary camp. But trail excavations showed that it had been a more permanent installation, for along with a 3.4m wide, V-shaped primary ditch, they also revealed timber structures and a road in the interior, whilst subsequent air photographs have also shown faint traces of a *principia*. The easiest interpretation was

31   Burgh-by-Sands III from the south-east

1 Ardoch Roman fort from the air. DJW

2 Kaims Castle fortlet. DJW

3   Cargill Roman fortlet Perthshire. DJW

4   Corbridge from the south-east. DJW

5   *Warden Hill Iron Age hillfort from the south-east*

6   *Vindolanda from the south-east*. DJW

7   *Carvoran from the north.* DJW

8   *Old Church Brampton fort from the north-west*

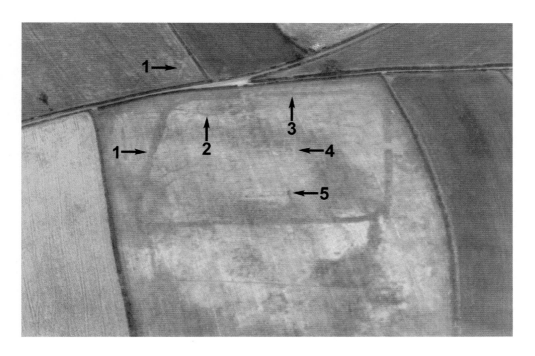

9   Burgh-by-Sands fort I from the north-west. Reproduced by kind permission of P.S. Austin

10   Milecastle 48 from the south-west

11 Turret 35a from the north. DJW

12 Chesters bridge and baths from the north-east. DJW

13 *South Shields fort from the north-east.* DJW

14 *South Shields fort gate reconstruction from the west.* DJW

15   *Wallsend fort from the south-east.* DJW

16   *Halton Chesters from the north-east*

17 *Chesters fort from the east.* DJW

18 *Chesters fort baths, from the south-east.* DJW

19   *Milecastle 29 from the north-east.* DJW

20   *Carrawburgh fort from the north.* DJW

21   Milecastle 35 from the north. DJW

22   Housesteads from the south. DJW

23   *Housesteads from the north-east.* DJW

24   *Milecastle 37 from the north-west.* DJW

25   Milecastle 42 from the north-east. DJW

26   Milking Gap native farmstead from the north-west with the Vallum beyond

27 *Great Chesters from the north.*
DJW

28 *Willowford Roman bridge and*
milecastle 49 from the north-east.
DJW

29   *Birdoswald fort from the south.* DJW

30   *Risingham fort from the north-east.* DJW

31 *Bewcastle fort from the north.* DJW

32 *Birrens fort from the south-east*

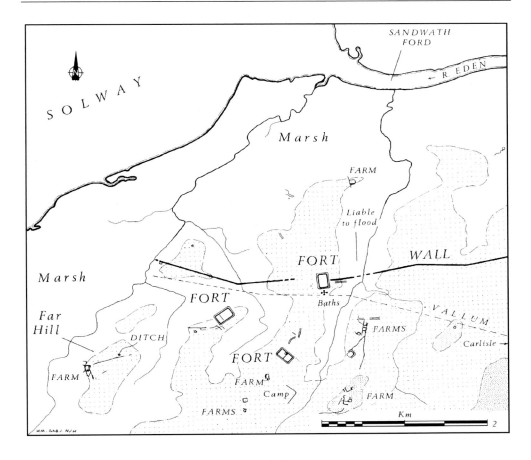

32 *Map of Roman and native sites around Burgh-by-Sands*

thus to associate the site with the construction of the Wall in the area and/or to suggest that it was designed as an early support for a potential weak spot, namely the possible break in the Wall caused by the nearby Burgh Marsh sector, which the Wall reaches but is not known to have crossed. However, now that the Wall fort itself seems to have been a significantly later addition to the line, possibly as late as the third century (Austen 1994, 52f), we no longer need to fit both of these rearward forts into the Stanegate and/or very early Wall periods: one may only have come into garrison when the other was abandoned. This is currently impossible to prove, since the pottery recovered does not allow a closer dating than that fort III was occupied at some point in the first half of the second century. Indeed, it has to be admitted that the entire fort sequence at both new sites has not yet been established beyond doubt by the limited excavations performed, and the account given here is merely the most likely scenario on current evidence. It remains possible that the forts were extended, rather than reduced, during their operational lives, and at Burgh-by-Sands I it is not even certain that the area to the east of the modern road is not an annex.

Two other large overlapping enclosures, which may be temporary camps, have also been located from the air to the south of fort III, and parts of both are visible at the bottom left-hand corner of **31**. In addition, aerial reconnaissance has revealed numerous native farms in the area, which seem likely to be broadly contemporary with the Roman period and, although space precludes our including air photographs of these, they have been mapped on **32**.

Kirkbride fort, NY 221574

It has long been known that there was a substantial Roman site at Kirkbride, at a point close to the River Wampool, just before it enters Moricambe. Finds recovered from the spot dated it to the early second century AD and the potential of its location as a coastal terminus for the emerging western Stanegate made it seem certain that a fort would eventually be found (Birley and Bellhouse 1963). There were no surface indications, however, and the Roman finds came from such a large area that, although several seasons of patient excavation led by R.L. Bellhouse were able to confirm the fort's existence, its exact size and layout proved surprisingly difficult to pin down (Bellhouse & Richardson 1975). Fortunately, in the severe drought year of 1976, air photography was finally able to be of some assistance, and a picture of the area revealed a fort's main internal east-west and north-south roads (**33**, arrows 1 & 2). Using this information, Bellhouse and Richardson (1982) were able to design excavations which gave a much fuller picture of the site and proved that it occupied the best possible point in the vicinity: a low ridge with a reasonable field of view.

More aerial discoveries were to come. For some time later, a remarkable pattern of crop marks (**34**) showed the site to be both more complex and more extensive than had

33   *Kirkbride fort from the west*

34   Kirkbride fort and possible compound from the south

been thought. The picture again shows the fort's north-south road (arrow 1), this time running for quite some distance to the north, along with the north-eastern quadrant of its defensive ditch (arrow 2), something that had not been seen in 1976. It also, however, shows a wholly unexpected enclosure (arrow 3) to the north of the fort. No excavation has yet been carried out on this new feature and thus its nature cannot be established with any confidence. But it has the rectangular form with rounded corners of a Roman military installation and may well be a temporary camp or a separate compound of some kind. It might even be an earlier or later fort, although the air photograph makes its surrounding ditch appear rather too narrow for that.

The running defences

In addition to its forts, the western Stanegate has also revealed signs of a running barrier, something the rest of the system still seems to lack. This takes the form of lengths of a substantial V-shaped ditch, running immediately to the north of the road (which has its own flanking drainage ditches), and which in places has been proved by excavation to be fronted by a timber palisade or fence. At present two main lengths of this ditch have been found from the air and although there may well be others still awaiting discovery, those known so far run across areas of slightly higher dry ground in a sector which was largely moss land in ancient times. In other words, they sealed off possible corridors for movement from the Solway into the interior. The longer of the two sections lies on

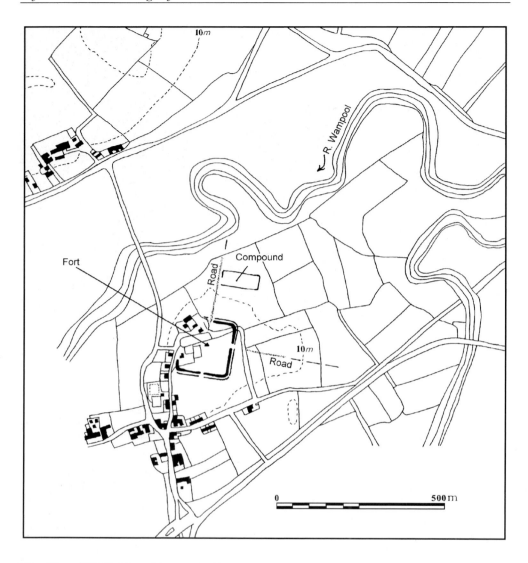

35   Plan of Kirkbride and its surroundings

Fingland Rigg (NY 2657) where over a mile has come to light over successive flying seasons (**36**, arrow 1), whilst a shorter stretch, still close to half a mile in length (**37**), is known at Farhill (NY 303581).

Fingland Rigg has, since its discovery, proved to be an object lesson in the potential dangers of using air photographic data without the follow-up of fieldwork on the ground. Firstly, some of the earliest air photographs of the sector showed a rectilinear enclosure with rounded corners which was initially interpreted as another possible fort. It later proved to be of native origin, but soon afterwards a roughly circular feature came to light which was actually intersected by the running ditch and which seemed likely to be the

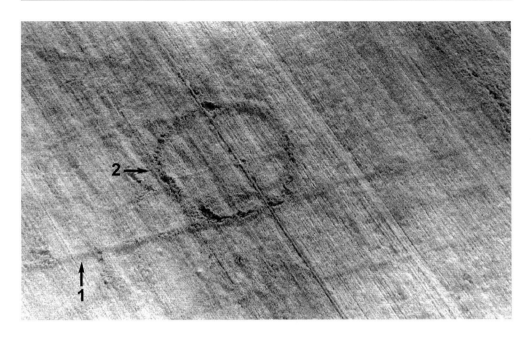

36   *The Roman running ditch on Fingland Rigg passing the watch tower at Easton*

37   *The Roman running ditch on Farhill*

ditch of a Roman watchtower. The site was excavated on this expectation in 1973 (Richardson 1977), but it too proved to be native, probably a small farmstead. Nevertheless, it did seem likely that genuine watchtowers would have existed in this area, especially after the discovery of the example underlying the fort of Burgh-by-Sands I, and two such installations have indeed now come to light. The first is at Farhill (NY 302582), which is intervisible with the Burgh I tower and also with the next new discovery at Easton (**36**, arrow 2) (NY 278579), which would have allowed signalling links over most of the distance between Burgh and Kirkbride. Easton itself could have been linked to Kirkbride by means of one more tower, again on Finland Rigg, a superb observation position that also has the more southerly fort of Old Carlisle in view (**38**). A tower at this point would explain too an apparent oddity in the position of Easton, which is situated further north than one might have expected, on low ground beneath the ridge along which the Stanegate and its ditch run, and thus has a much more restricted field of view. This situation would simply have been an economy measure because, as presently sited, Easton is able to see around the north side of a bend in Finland Rigg to that part of the hill which also has Kirkbride in view, whereas the ridge top to its south, despite its higher elevation, does not. Thus yet another tower would have been needed to link the two. Sadly, however, if there was a tower on Finland Rigg, it remains undiscovered. For, as we have seen, the only likely crop mark so far recorded has now been shown to be a native farmstead and, for the moment at least, it still remains unclear how (or indeed if)

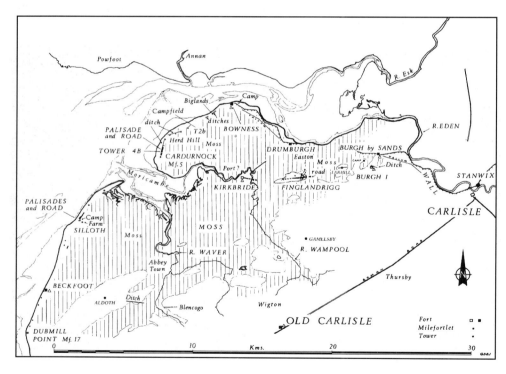

38   Map of the western Stanegate and Cumberland Coast

Kirkbride was linked to the rest of the line. Further east, Burgh I and Carlisle are both intervisible with a point at Monkhill (NY 344582), where a faint penannular crop mark may show the remains of a tower (now largely destroyed by a modern building). Alternatively, there is another faint ring feature some 800m further east at Kirkandrews-on-Eden (NY 350585), at a point with a better view of Carlisle, which may also be a tower.

Even this might not be the whole story, however, for air photography is now beginning to reveal what might be a second line of ditches and towers about 5km further to the south, between Old Carlisle fort and Beckfoot on the coast (**38**). Again, two long stretches of ditch are known, this time without an accompanying road. They stretch for a total of over a mile in the area to the west of Blencogo (**38**), and beyond the western end of this sector a tower was found from the air at Aldoth (NY 136485) on a high point overlooking the coast. It is possible that this second line might also run to the north-east from Blencogo, following the higher ground, and it could stretch some distance inland. There have been further air photographic indications of linear ditches to the north of Old Carlisle, and yet another timber watchtower has now been discovered from the air (and later excavated) at Gamelsby (NY 269523), about halfway between Old Carlisle and Fingland Rigg. As with all of these towers, it was initially identified by the circular crop mark of its ditch (**39**, arrowed), but unlike the others it was found to have an associated square feature (visible on **39** just to the right of the ring ditch), which may have been an external barrack or guard house. Such structures are currently very rare on Roman towers, but possibly only because excavators seldom look outside their ditches. At least one other is known: at Garnhall tower on the Antonine Wall in Scotland (Woolliscroft, forthcoming (a)).

39   The Roman tower at Gamelsby from the north-west

Old Carlisle (Latin name probably Maglona), NY 259465

Given its location, backing the emerging second defensive line behind the western Stanegate, it is tempting to wonder whether Old Carlisle might have been occupied in this early period. Unfortunately, although (or possibly because) the site is superbly preserved, it has never been subjected to even small scale excavation. Its date thus remains something of a mystery. The site has yielded a reasonable body of inscriptions but, as is often the case, these all relate to occupation in the late second and early third centuries and only excavation is likely to detect any earlier activity (Birley 1951). The inscriptions do, however, allow us to identify a later garrison: a cavalry unit called the *Ala Augusta ob Virtutem Appellata* (literally 'the Emperor's own squadron, so called because of its courage'), a slightly unusual title in that it does not contain a number. This highly mobile unit, coupled to good road communications, would have allowed the fort to act as a strategic reserve for the whole of the western end of Hadrian's Wall and its flanking defences on the Cumberland coast; this was probably its main function.

Figure **40** shows the four and a half acre fort standing on a promontory, overlooking the Wiza Beck and, although the site remains unexcavated, a certain amount of internal detail can be made out. In particular, the street grid remains visible and in low light the remains of buildings can be discerned through the trenches dug when their walls were robbed of their stone for later farm and field wall construction. Outside the fort, similar robber trenches provide an even clearer picture of a substantial civil settlement flanking both the main Roman road from Carlisle to the coast (**40**, arrow 1), and a branch road (arrow 2) which heads for the fort's east gate (from which a road to the north is also

40   *Old Carlisle from the east*

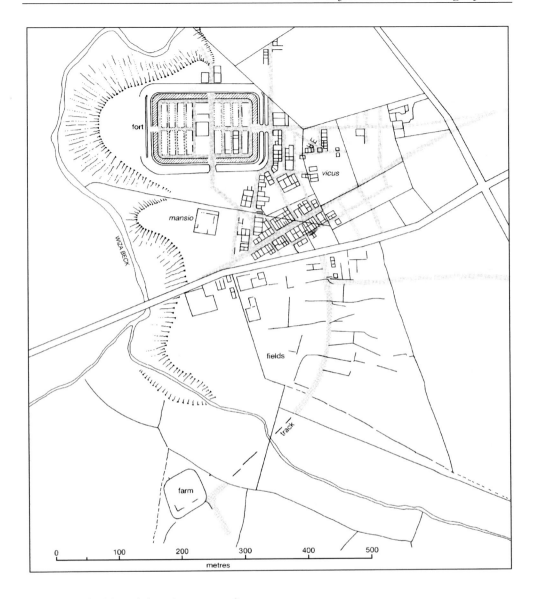

41   Plan of Old Carlisle and its surroundings

known to have radiated). Other structures are known to the north and east of the fort and the individual buildings have been plotted in as great a detail as air photographs currently allow in **41**.

In addition to the fort and its immediate *vicus*, block flying of the entire area has revealed a complex of associated field systems, farmsteads and trackways that formed part of the fabric of the surrounding Roman-British countryside. These peripheral features, some of which are shown in **41**, appear to be in a native architectural/agricultural

73

tradition, but were linked into the Roman road system and to the fort itself. To some extent, therefore, they reveal the integration (albeit limited) that developed between the two cultures, along with the combined stimulus given to the native economy by the Roman road network, the logistical needs of its attendant forts and the security brought by the frontier.

This, then, is our present understanding of the pre-mural development of the Tyne-Solway frontier and we may now turn to the constituent elements of Hadrian's Wall itself.

3 Hadrian's Wall

History and development

The Stanegate was a powerful system, but it was still primarily an invasion defence, dependant on large concentrations of force which could rapidly be combined to form a substantial army, backed ultimately by the legions stationed further south. The road itself would, no doubt, have been patrolled and the fortlets and towers would have allowed reasonably tight visual surveillance, but the Stanegate was still an open frontier. It would thus have been relatively easy for small raiding parties and the like to cross it unobserved, especially in poor weather or at night, and it was to combat these sorts of low intensity threats that Hadrian's Wall was built in the AD 120s.

With the decision to construct the Wall we reach much firmer historical ground than was the case with the development of the Stanegate. A key event was probably the visit of the Emperor Hadrian to Britain in AD 122 as part of his review of the outlying provinces of the Empire. He had spent the years immediately prior to his accession in AD 117 involved in the eastern campaigns of his predecessor Trajan. Their near chaotic aftermath (involving widespread rebellions) must have made him aware of the necessity of stabilising the frontiers, even if that involved (as it did in the east) the abandonment of territory gained by military conquest. As with his slightly earlier visit to Germany, his period in Britain thus led to a new frontier infrastructure.

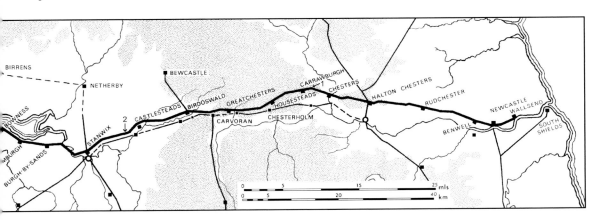

42 *Map of Hadrian's Wall.* Reproduced by kind permission of D.J. Breeze

75

The Wall stretched for 80 Roman miles from Wallsend on the Tyne to Bowness-on-Solway (although the section from Wallsend to Newcastle seems to have been a slightly later addition) and ran, for the most part, on higher ground a little to the north of the line followed by the Stanegate. Along the central sector, in particular, it took advantage of the prominent north-facing volcanic scarp called the Whin Sill, which runs from Carrawburgh to Carvoran and offered both tactical strength and long range views to the north (**43**). In the popular imagination the system is often seen as being constructed by slave or forced civilian labour, but inscriptions offer ample evidence for its construction by the army itself. Indeed, most of the work was done by the elite, Roman citizen, legionary troops and not by the auxiliaries who were to man it.

Like the Stanegate, the Wall did not develop in a single structural phase. The original design suffered frequent changes during construction, and its building sequence has provided a fascinating puzzle for archaeologists as each modification left subtle traces in the fabric of the finished product. The process was so complex in places that at least one book has been written entirely about it (Stevens 1966), although more recent work (e.g. Crow 1991) has shown that the individual developmental stages may have been rather more jumbled together than had once been thought.

As originally conceived, the Wall was to be a relatively simple, if grandiose, structure. Firstly, there was the Wall itself. It is known to have been built from east to west and was begun at a gauge of 10ft thick, although parts of it were later finished to narrower gauges. It is thought to have stood in the region of 15ft high, although no section now stands taller than 11ft, and there is limited evidence that it may have carried a patrol walk and parapet along its top. It consisted of a clay and rubble or concrete and rubble core, faced with roughly dressed masonry, and stood on a foundation of flagstones. For some unexplained reason, although the first 49 Roman miles from the Tyne to the Irthing were built in stone from the start, the westernmost 31 miles from the Irthing to the Solway were initially built of turf and replaced in stone later, in some places perhaps as late as the late second or early third century. In front of both the stone and turf Walls was a massive V-shaped ditch 30ft or so across and 10ft deep, which was often cut straight through extremely hard volcanic rock and now tends to survive better than the Wall itself.

In addition to the Wall and ditch, the system also carried a series of small fortifications. At intervals of approximately one Roman mile it was pierced by gateways guarded by small fortlets (about 20m square internally), which we now call milecastles. There are 80 Roman miles of Wall and so there should have been 80 milecastles; the positions of all but a few in urban areas have now been established. As an aid to navigation on the Wall archaeologists use a numbering system in which these installations are numbered off from the east, so that milecastle (MC) 1 is in Wallsend and MC 80 just outside Bowness. Hadrian's Wall should not be pictured as some form of vast scaled up version of a city wall, designed to withstand major assaults. It was too lightly manned to be defensible against a serious invasion. Nor was it an early version of the Berlin Wall, for it was never designed to be uncrossable. It remained vital that the army should be able to pass through it freely, if only for simple maintenance purposes, and it was also important that civilian traffic, trade and perhaps transhumance could continue, not least because of the tax revenue to be gained from customs duties paid at the frontiers by civilians. The Wall was simply designed to make illicit crossings more difficult, whilst channelling legitimate traffic towards recognised crossing places, and it was the milecastle gateways that allowed these movements. They were frequent enough to present no serious inconvenience and yet secure enough to allow close scrutiny of travellers and their goods.

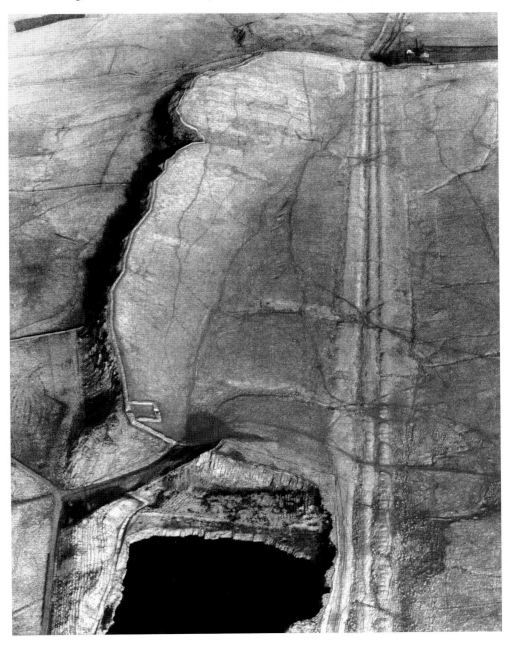

43   Hadrian's Wall with milecastle 42 from the west, with the Vallum to the rear

Figure **43** shows an air photograph of Cawfields milecastle (NY 716667), in the central sector, near to the Stanegate fortlet of Haltwhistle Burn. This is MC 42, and is thus 42 Roman miles west of Wallsend. Hadrian's Wall is visible running along the ridge top to the east of (beyond) the site, but just to the west a long section of the remains have been destroyed by Cawfields quarry. No internal buildings have survived at MC 42, but **colour plate 10** shows the better preserved MC 48 beside the Poltross Burn in Gilsland, on the border between Cumbria and Northumberland (NY 634663). The milecastle is shown to be a fairly simple structure. The defences are clearly visible just to the east (right) of the modern Carlisle to Newcastle railway and the front and rear gates can be seen to have massive foundations which almost certainly carried towers, perhaps up to 10m in height. The fortlet had a road running through it, on either side of which are two narrow rectangular buildings (there is sometimes just one). These are usually interpreted as barracks, although there is no proof of this, and they may also have served as customs offices and the like. If they were barracks, however, being roughly the same size as individual fort contubernia (see appendix) they should have held eight men each. In the north-western (top left) corner a stone oven where the soldiers cooked their rations is just visible, whilst in the north-eastern corner, a flight of stone steps can be seen leading up to the Wall top. These stairs are now badly damaged so that their highest surviving step still lies well short of the milecastle's side wall. But we can use the height and depth of the extant steps to project the point at which they would have met the fortlet wall and it is this that allows us at least to approximate the original height of Hadrian's Wall.

On the stone Wall, the milecastles have stone built defences and internal buildings, but on the turf sector both were of turf and timber, although they were rebuilt in stone at the same time as the Wall itself.

Between each of the milecastles was a pair of towers, generally referred to as turrets. They were set slightly into the body of the Wall and were built of stone from the start, even on the turf Wall. Again they would probably have stood about 10m high and, as no roof tiles have been found amongst their ruins, they may have had flat crenellated roofs. Their role was to act as observation platforms from which a lookout could be mounted over the entire frontier and, along with the milecastle towers, this gave a watch point every third of a Roman mile (470m). This is about twice the tower density of the Gask system and many times that of the Stanegate, and is unusually high even when compared to contemporary systems around the Empire.

The turrets are incorporated into the milecastle numbering system, being counted off as turret a and b from the milecastle to their east so, for example, we would have MC 1 then T 1a, T 1b and then MC 2 etc. In many ways this might be a misrepresentation of the original design, for the Romans more probably saw the arrangement of each Wall mile as a milecastle flanked by two towers, rather than one milecastle followed by two towers. But, as the numbers are only intended as a cataloguing system, this probably does not matter unduly. Colour plate 11 shows T 35a (NY 801701) atop the Whin Sill crags in the central sector. Again, the turrets are very simple installations, with a single entrance doorway in the rear wall and often an internal stone platform to act as the base for a ladder to give access to the upper levels.

Finally, the Wall crosses three major rivers, the North Tyne, the Irthing and the Eden and here substantial bridges were built to carry first the patrol walk, and later possibly the Wall itself. Colour plate 12 shows the eastern abutment of the North Tyne bridge (NY 915701) at Chesters fort. The structure is visible to the left of the river and, although partly obscured by trees, it is immediately apparent that its basically triangular ground plan is very like that of a modern bridge abutment. The feature has now been left high and dry by a drift of the river to the west, but the opposite abutment and the intervening support piers can still occasionally be seen in the river when the water is either low or particularly clear. A small section of the Wall can be seen approaching the abutment from the east (left) and meeting the bridge itself at a square tower. The abutment also contains a stone culvert which may have led water to a mill wheel. Like all of the Hadrian's Wall bridges, the Chesters example is built of superbly dressed masonry of a very much higher quality than that used in the Wall itself. Bridge construction may, therefore, have involved special, more highly skilled, masons.

Initially this simple, lightly manned layout was all that was envisaged and the Wall was designed, and to a large extent built, on the assumption that the main invasion defences would remain in the old Stanegate forts, which all lay between a few hundred metres and a mile or two to the south. The Wall was thus seen as a thickening of the old system and not as a replacement for it. It was in effect a labour saving device, to give greatly enhanced border control with the least possible dispersal of manpower. Before this initial design was even completed, however, the frontier was subjected to a major reworking in which sections of finished Wall and even a few milecastles and turrets were demolished and a completely new series of (eventually) 15 forts was slotted in to replace all but three of the old Stanegate bases. We are not sure of the reasons for this move; perhaps the Wall had simply been inconveniencing military movements. But, for the first time, the main invasion defence units now came to lie on the line of the Wall itself. Colour plate 12 shows part of the Wall fort of Chesters (along with its external bath building) visible on the opposite bank of the North Tyne from the bridge abutment, and we will deal with others in more detail below. Where the terrain allowed, the forts normally stood with their short axes parallel to the Wall and often with the forward third of their normally six-gated layout projecting beyond the line. But at some points, such as Housesteads fort (see below), the steep scarp of the Whin Sill prevented this and the fort was attached to the rear of the line with its long axis parallel to the Wall. Like their Stanegate predecessors, the Wall forts were manned by non-Roman auxiliary troops. But although there is a tendency to regard these units as second rate when compared with the elite citizen legions, they were still highly trained soldiers and extremely effective fighting forces.

The forts did not exist in a vacuum, for there were plenty of civilians in the Wall area. Units of up to 1,000 well-paid soldiers stationed in often isolated positions represented a significant pool of spending power and, like the Stanegate forts, all of the Wall forts rapidly attracted little towns (known as vici) of civilian traders eager to provide the often dubious, wine, women and song-oriented services for which frontier towns have always been known. These settlements often became quite prosperous, but they seem to have retained something of a Wild West atmosphere. Indeed, when one of the buildings of Housesteads' vicus was excavated it was found to be some sort of bar which had what was obviously a murder victim buried under its floor, with part of a knife blade still embedded in its ribs. The vici did have their higher side, however. There was a great deal of industrial activity, including metal working and the manufacture of pottery, glass and textiles. We find inscriptions set up by local councils, so some of them, at least, seem to have had a form of local government. There was also spiritual life: temples of one sort or another are common, dedicated to various gods. Mithras, a Persian deity, was popular with the later Roman army. Roman gods such as Jupiter and the war god Mars were worshipped and more local Celtic gods were also popular, for example Antenociticus, who had a temple at Benwell fort. There are even signs that Christian churches may have been emerging by the very late Roman period, something hitherto conspicuous by its absence. But it may still be the case that the northern frontier remained obstinately pagan until long after the heart lands of the Empire had turned to Christianity. There were also official buildings in the towns, such as *mansiones*, which were imperial posting stations and guesthouses for visiting officials, and of course we have the ubiquitous Roman bath blocks which were really military buildings, built outside the forts to reduce their inherent fire risk.

Finally, although Roman soldiers were not allowed to marry, at least before the third century, they still frequently established long-term relationships. This meant that, although the men were compelled to live in barracks, their women would often settle in the vicus, and their children often formed part of the next generation of recruits. Tombstones set up by members of these couples show that, once the man had completed his military service, they would often marry and settle down locally and so there would also be veterans in the town.

The next addition to the Wall is unique anywhere in the Empire. It is a huge flat-bottomed, steep-sided ditch, 20ft wide and 10ft deep. This is flanked on either side by an earth rampart 20ft wide and set back 30ft from the ditch, which makes the feature 120ft (37m) wide in all. In places a low extra mound, often called the 'marginal mound', is visible immediately to the south of the ditch and for years this was thought to be a secondary feature produced by periodic cleaning of the ditch to remove silts. Recent work by A. Wilmott near Birdoswald fort has shown it to be part of the original design, however, although its function is currently unclear.

The modern name for the monument is the Vallum. In many ways this is a misnomer since vallum is latin for rampart and the dominant surviving feature of this structure is its ditch, but it has become the official term and there would be little point in changing it now. The Vallum runs behind the Wall, usually immediately behind it, although it occasionally wanders up to half a mile further south. We know that it is contemporary with or later than most of the forts, because it deviates to avoid them but, like the forts, it predates Hadrian's death in 138. In places, the Vallum is so well preserved that it can be the most striking surviving element of the Wall system and a particularly good stretch can be seen on **43** to the south (right) of MC 42. Elsewhere, however, it is only really visible from the air. Colour plate 12, which was shot against the light, shows its ditch visible as a faint shadow mark (arrowed) as it approaches the fort of Chesters where, unusually, it appears to fall in with the fort's rear ditch, rather than deviating past the south of the site.

The Vallum is truly colossal and must have changed the way in which the Wall worked, because it could only be crossed at special fortified causeways at the forts and so denied access to the milecastles from the south. What purpose it served still remains something of a mystery for, although almost every archaeologist who has worked on the Wall has offered suggestions, there is currently no conclusive evidence. One thing is certain however: the old idea, still occasionally to be seen in the literature, that it was a second line of defence to protect the Wall from a possibly still restive native population to the south can no longer be supported. Even supposing that the Romans could have manned such a defence, it must be must remembered that the monument has a rampart on both sides and no defensive force would build a ready made rampart on its enemy's side for him to hide behind. Besides, the Vallum often follows a very weak tactical line, so much so that in a number of places it is overlooked by cliffs immediately to its south where, in an age without firearms, a gang of children with catapults could have beaten the best army in the world off its ramparts.

Another popular theory has seen the Vallum as a demarcation line for a military zone to the rear of the Wall which was closed to civilians. It would thus form a conspicuous marker rather than an uncrossable barrier: a line that no one might cross without good reason but which, at the same time, no one could cross without noticing. The main weakness of this theory is the sheer scale of the work, however. It is hard to see what it would have achieved in this largely symbolic role that could not have been done far more easily by a reasonably sturdy fence. A more plausible idea might be that the Vallum was the Roman equivalent of a tank trap, because although it would have been possible to scramble across it on foot, its very steep sided ditch would have made it quite unsurmountable for horses and cattle. As raiders in Roman times, just like the medieval border reivers of the same area, were probably horsemen trying to steal cattle; the presence of the Vallum would ensure that anyone wanting to force a crossing of the Wall would have to hit it at a fort, the strongest points, because these had the only crossings. As seen today, the milecastles do not have any provision for getting across the Wall's own ditch and so they might seem to have been reasonably well defended (and relatively pointless) anyway. But recent work has shown that they may originally have had causeways across the ditch, which were later dug out (Welfare 2000). If so, they could have seemed too vulnerable and the Vallum may have been installed as a backstop to seal the line further.

What happened next on the Wall was largely the result of internal Roman politics. Hadrian was childless and his first choice of successor predeceased him. As a replacement, Hadrian picked on a teenaged Marcus Aurelius. But as the Emperor was already ailing and the boy was still too young to succeed him directly, Hadrian selected a little known, but similarly childless, middle-aged politician called Antoninus as a stop gap successor, likely to live just long enough for Aurelius to grow up. In fact, Antoninus ruled for over 20 years and presided over one of the most peaceful and prosperous periods in the Empire's history. Yet as an unknown with little of the military charisma that was so vital to Roman political kudos, his initial position was precarious and he sought to establish himself by winning glory, just as the Emperor Claudius had with the original invasion of Britain. The result was that, in the early 140s, Hadrian's Wall was totally abandoned; southern Scotland was reoccupied and an entirely new, much shorter Wall was built between Carriden on the Forth and Old Kilpatrick

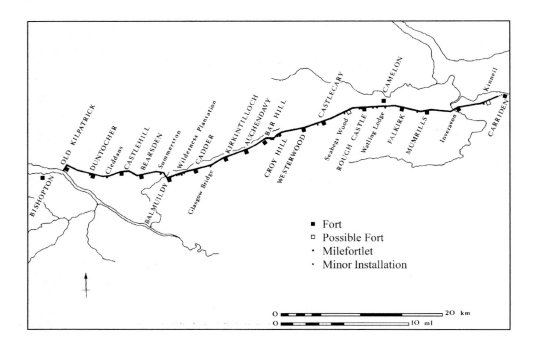

44 *Map of the Antonine Wall.* Drawn by H. McBrien and reproduced by kind permission of the Glasgow Archaeological Society

on the Clyde. Unfortunately, the province was not given any new forces to cope with this expansion and so the Antonine Wall suffered the same problems as Agricola's conquests had 60 years before, when Legio II Adiutrix was pulled out. The move was thus short lived. At latest, when Aurelius did finally become Emperor in AD 161, he ordered a withdrawal of the frontier back to Hadrian's Wall, where it remained for the rest of the Roman period. Indeed, a case can be made for an abandonment under Antoninus himself, in the late 150s.

The initial design of the Antonine Wall seems to have been very similar to that reached by Hadrian's Wall at the time of its abandonment, except that this time the whole of the line was constructed of turf (albeit laid on a stone foundation). There was the Wall itself, which may only have been slightly lower than Hadrian's Wall, despite its turf construction, and there was an often much larger ditch. A series of large auxiliary forts, now called the primary forts, was constructed, attached to the rear of the barrier. Indeed, two of these, Balmuildy and Castlecary, were build of stone and, more significantly, had stone wing walls projecting from their northern corners as if to meet an Antonine Wall that was originally expected to be built in stone. Lastly, a system of turf and timber milecastles has been emerging over the last few decades such as the example shown in **45** (arrow 1). The site lies on Golden Hill, Duntocher (NS 496726) towards the western end of the Wall, and is visible on the air photograph by the stone foundation of its turf walls, which were excavated between 1948 and 1951 (Robertson 1957, 16ff). Unusually, this fortlet was later incorporated into a small fort, which is not visible on the photograph. The

45   The Antonine Wall milefortlet at Duntocher from the north-west

Wall ditch is faintly visible descending the hill (arrow 2), as is a small section of the Wall's own foundation, now protected by a square of iron railings (arrow 3).

Despite their similarities, there were two important differences in the layout of the two Walls. Firstly, there are as yet few signs that the Antonine Wall had a tower system akin to Hadrian's Wall's turrets. A number of small features are known that may have served a similar purpose, but they are very varied and not well enough understood to form a coherent picture. For example, just to the east of Balmuildy fort (**44**), three small semicircular ditches have been detected (from the air) at one-sixth Roman mile intervals, projecting from the rear of the Wall around the milefortlet of Wilderness Plantation. It was originally thought that these were defences for timber towers set into the back of the Wall. The only one to be properly excavated proved to be empty, however, and so their function remains uncertain. Further east, around Croy Hill and Rough Castle forts, three pairs of turf expansions are known which are often described as beacon stances, and an additional example is now known at Inveravon. Again, however, we cannot honestly say that we know what these were for. Finally, recent work at Garnhall, just to the west of Castlecary fort, found a normal Roman timber watchtower with a ring ditch, just like the Gask examples, immediately south of the Wall (Woolliscroft forthcoming, (a)). But no more such towers have yet come to light, and there is no sign of any of these installation types forming a regular series. For the moment, therefore, the entire question of a turret system must remain open, except to say that if the Wall does not have a tower chain of some sort, it will be unique amongst all of Rome's known frontiers.

The Antonine Wall also has no equivalent of the Vallum, but then neither does any other frontier elsewhere in the Roman world. Indeed whatever Hadrian's Wall's Vallum was meant to achieve, it may have proved either a failure or, at least, unnecessary. It was slighted when the army moved north, by the laying of frequent earth causeways across its ditch, only some of which were removed again when the Wall was reoccupied. In some stretches it was eventually filled in altogether; for example, Housesteads fort's third-century vicus buildings completely overlie the buried Vallum ditch.

Like Hadrian's Wall, the Antonine Wall was subjected to a major redesign whilst still under construction. As we have seen, the Wall had major forts at about the same six Roman mile interval as Hadrian's Wall. The Antonine Wall was only half the length, however, which meant that although its force density was the same as the southern Wall, it had only half the total garrison. This obviously came to be seen as insufficient for almost immediately a series of secondary forts was slotted in between the primaries, to bring the inter-fort interval down to sometimes less than two miles. Ten of these secondary forts are known at present and a further two are suspected (compared to only six primaries) but they are often much smaller than the primary forts and may not have been able to hold a complete auxiliary unit. We have already mentioned Duntocher fort, but **46** (arrow 1) shows the best preserved example, at Rough Castle, Falkirk (NX 844798), which is only a little over an acre in area. The air photograph was taken in summer when trees obscure parts of the site, but the ditch and rampart circuit of the fort, including its four entrance breaks, can be seen, with the defences of a slightly larger annex beyond. In front of the

46   *The Antonine Wall fort of Rough Castle from the west*

fort, the ditch of the Antonine Wall is clearly visible running through the picture (arrow 2), with the Wall itself, in a rare state of preservation, forming the fort's north rampart. To the north (left) of the Wall ditch, a series of small pits laid out in quincunx formation can be made out as an area of black dots (arrow 3). These are *lilia*, the Roman equivalent to land mines: pit traps which would once have contained upward-pointing sharpened steaks. They would have been covered with vegetation to conceal them and formed a reasonably deep defensive band so that any attacker trying to approach the fort would be almost bound to fall into one and be impaled. For many years these features were thought to be unique to Rough Castle, but recently they have been found in a number of other places on both the Antonine Wall and, still more recently, Hadrian's Wall, and so may prove to be a more general part of the frontier defences. All of the other discoveries have been made slightly further back, on the berm between the Wall ditches and the Walls themselves, and so Rough Castle's forward lilia remain exceptional. Yet little or no work has been done ahead of either line elsewhere to look for parallels.

The exact abandonment date of the Antonine Wall is not known with certainty. It was once thought to have survived for much of the rest of the second century, but an end date of around 160 or even in the late 150s now appears more likely. Whatever the case, Hadrian's Wall was refurbished for renewed **use and** at least some of the Vallum causeways were removed. It is also usually, though not universally, thought that the final major element was added to the Hadrian's Wall system at this point. So far the Wall had relied for its lateral communications on the old Stanegate road which might lie anywhere between a few hundred metres and several miles to its south. This obviously came to be seen as insufficient, however, for a completely new road was now built along the Wall's entire length, which we call the Military Way. This might have been a rare example of Hadrian's Wall copying the Antonine Wall (rather than vice versa), which had needed such a road, since it lacked any previously installed equivalent to the Stanegate. Whatever the case, the Military Way is a superb piece of engineering. It never strays far from the line and often runs right behind it. Yet by means of a few minor course changes and the judicious use of cuttings and embankments it manages, even in the rough central sector, to follow far gentler gradients than the often roller-coaster course of the Wall itself. What became the final configuration of the line can be seen in **47**. The air photograph shows the Wall approaching Limestone Corner, its northernmost point, from the east (c.NY 880715). The Wall itself can be seen running down the centre of the picture, largely as a broad, linear robber trench (arrow 1), with the ditch to its north (right). In the foreground, the foundations of T 29b are clearly visible as a pale square (arrow 2), whilst MC 30 is faintly detectable in the distance (arrow 3). Outside the line, low sunlight has thrown a series of low mounds into stark relief; these represent dumps of upcast from the digging of the Wall ditch, whilst behind the Wall the Military Way can be made out as a faint running mound (arrow 4). Finally, the Vallum can be seen towards the left of the picture, with the modern B 6318 running on its north rampart. The ditch, south rampart and marginal mound are all clearly visible to the left of the road (arrow 5), with clear signs of the regular crossings cut during the Antonine Wall period and never subsequently removed.

Finally, complex as it was, the Wall cannot be seen in isolation. It was just one element in a vast system of frontier control totalling over 400 separate installations. There were

47   *Hadrian's Wall east of Limestone Corner from the south-east*

outposts to the north and a line of defences down the Cumberland coast. The latter were augmented by towers down the Yorkshire coast much later, in the fourth century, and behind the Wall lay a network of roads, additional forts and smaller installations stretching all the way back to the legionary bases of York, Chester and Caerleon. Furthermore, although the building of the Military Way marks the end of the Wall's development, it was by no means the end of its history. It continued to be manned right down to the very end of Roman Britain in the early fifth century and, even then, it was abandoned by Rome, not defeated. Indeed there are signs that occupation of some sort continued even longer. In a way, like all Rome's frontiers, it was a massive monument to the failure of the old idea of *imperium sine fine* and, specifically, to Rome's failure to conquer the entire island of Britain. But on its own terms it was a spectacular success. For it guaranteed the safety of its province almost without interruption for 300 years, a track record unmatched by any other Roman frontier.

The sites

South Shields (Latin name probably Arbeia), NX 365679

Amid the industrial areas of Tyneside still linger traces of the past, which are now being brought vividly back into the light by the long term excavation programs run by Tyne and Wear Museums. The eastern end of the Wall system, though not the Wall itself, ultimately rested on the fort at South Shields, which overlooked the mouth of the Tyne estuary from the south. At first sight the survival of archaeological remains in such a context might appear unlikely but in fact, industrialised areas built up in the nineteenth century can sometimes preserve earlier features relatively intact. This is certainly the case at South Shields, where a laudable decision by the local authority has led to the permanent display of the remains of the Roman fort whose playing card shape is clearly visible in **colour plate 13**. In excavations prior to the Second World War part of the central area of the site was cleared of the overlying industrial housing and consolidated. Far more has been done in recent years, including the clearance of most of the remaining modern buildings, the creation of an on-site museum, a continuing excavation program and the in situ restoration of one of the fort's gates (**colour plate 14**) and part of the later commanding officer's residence (**colour plate 13**, 2).

The site was originally built under Antoninus as a relatively standard auxiliary fort, but in the early third century it was enlarged, and filled with no fewer than 22 granaries, identifiable from the air by their tell-tale buttresses (**colour plate 13**). Only the *principia* remained in its normal central position (**colour plate 13**, 1), whilst the *praetorium* and barracks were moved to the fort's south-east corner. This layout represents a most abnormal plan whose historical context was probably the northern campaigns of the Emperor Septimius Severus (AD 208-11). South Shields seems to have become the supply base for at least part of his campaigns into Scotland and presumably the army was provisioned from here by sea. After the campaigns, the fort was not restored to its original form, but continued to serve as a supply base for the Wall itself. This role is reflected in the personnel present on the site, for in addition to its main garrison, the 500 strong Coh

V Gallorum Equitata (and at some point a cavalry unit: the Ala I Hispanorum Asturum), we also have fourth-century records of a unit of Tigris lightermen, which shows an obvious concern with water transport.

Wallsend (Latin name Segedunum*) NX 300660*

In what is now the suburb of Wallsend, the easternmost section of Hadrian's Wall ran down from the terminal fort to the angle in the Tyne formed by the Long Reach and the Bill Reach. It was here, centuries later, that some of the great Tyneside shipyards were developed and the site of the Roman fort was dwarfed by the great cranes of the Swan Hunter yard. Archaeological interest in the site was stimulated when industrial housing began to engulf the site in the nineteenth century and the actual outline of the fort was established in 1929. Details of its junction with the Wall showed that the section east of Newcastle was an addition to the original design (which was not accompanied by the Vallum), perhaps made necessary in the later AD 120s or 30s by hostile infiltration across the Tyne estuary. Today, although a major road still bisects the site, the fort has been cleared of buildings. Fortunately, as at South Shields, the streets of former terraced housing did not have cellars and a remarkable amount of archaeological evidence has been proved to have survived. Large scale recent excavations were thus able to greatly amplify our knowledge of the site's history and, as can be seen in **colour plate 15**, the entire site has now been laid out as a visitor attraction with an excellent on-site museum.

The fort covered four acres, and had three gates projecting north of the Wall. It contained the usual central buildings, including a *principia* (**colour plate 15**, 1), *praetorium* (2) and double granary (3) along with a courtyard structure which is probably a small hospital (4). There were six barracks in the *praetentura* to the north (two of which are overlain by the modern Buddle Street) and four to the south (5). Inscriptions have shown that the garrison was the 500-strong second cohort of Nervians (from modern Belgium), followed in the third century and beyond by *Coh IV Lingonum*, from Germany. This second unit was part mounted and its presence has allowed the site to answer a long-standing puzzle for Roman military archaeologists, the question of how to recognise stables in Roman forts. In fact they have proved to be slightly modified versions of normal infantry barracks. The best examples are the two long buildings on either side of the numeral 5 in **colour plate 15**. The air photograph shows a series of oval brown dots, one to each of the *contubernia* front rooms in both buildings. Analysis of the soil in these features showed them to have been urine collection pits for horses and it would seem that these rooms were used as stables, whilst the rear rooms held the troopers themselves (Hodgson in Bidwell 1999, 86f).

The air photograph also shows a number of features outside the fort. Hadrian's Wall can be seen approaching from the west (**colour plate 15**, 6) and a small length just beside the modern road has been reconstructed to its estimated full original height. Just in front and to the right of this section, a series of tiny black dots can be made out on the berm between the Wall and its ditch. These are pit traps, similar to those already mentioned on the Antonine Wall, and another set have more recently been found on Byker Hill closer to Newcastle. As none have been found to the west of Newcastle these may prove to be a special provision made on this later eastern extension, perhaps to make up for the fact that the Vallum does not extend this far. But, as the berm has never seemed particularly worth excavating in the past, little attempt has been made to look for them elsewhere and so, for the moment, it seems best to reserve judgement.

The Wall met the fort in the west at a conventional point, just south of the main west gate but, in the east, the very final stretch of Wall down to the river leaves the fort, uniquely, at its south-east angle (**colour plate 15**, arrowed). To the west (left) of this terminal stretch, excavations have revealed signs of the fort's *vicus* which, unusually, was also defended by a wall leading back from Hadrian's Wall itself. Nothing is now visible of this settlement amongst a modern light industrial estate. But the new, red roofed structure visible in the bottom left-hand corner of the air photograph is a working reconstruction of the fort's bath house, in which the public will be able to enjoy the pleasures of Roman bathing.

Excavations have shown that major alterations took place in the third and fourth centuries, when the four southern barracks were rebuilt as so-called 'chalets'. Early Roman barrack blocks were single large buildings, subdivided to provide accommodation for an entire century or cavalry *turma*, but in these later structures each *contubernia* was built as a separate structure. These were separated from their neighbours by narrow eve drips so that, as the name suggests, each barrack came to resemble a row of small chalets. Similar barracks are known elsewhere on the Wall and we will see examples below at both Housesteads and Great Chesters. North of the main range, the early barracks were replaced by a collection of part-timber structures and more chalets, whilst possible stables came to fill other parts of the interior by the end of the fourth century. Many of these later structures were built from ephemeral materials: the recovery of so comprehensive and detailed a development sequence was a triumph of modern excavation techniques in the very difficult conditions of an industrial area.

Newcastle (Latin name Pons Aelius), NX 251638

Although there have been almost miraculous results from the built-up areas of South Shields and Wallsend, the same is only partly true of Newcastle upon Tyne. The fort (the old castle) lies in the heart of the modern city in an area now famous for its medieval castle (the new castle) and bridges across the Tyne. In the Roman period the site was unique on Hadrian's Wall in being named after the Emperor himself, for the Latin name *Pons Aelius* means 'bridge of Aelius' and Hadrian's full name was Publius Aelius Hadrianus. The presence of a modern city has naturally made it difficult to ascertain the precise layout of the fort (and the Wall in its vicinity). But parts of it have been uncovered in the castle area (**48**, arrowed), to the east of central station, and we know the names of two garrison units: *Coh I Ulpia Traiana Cugernorum*, in the early third century, and *Coh I Cornoviorum*, in the fourth. Both of these were 500-strong infantry units, with the Cornovi being, unusually, a unit of Britons, in an empire where, for security reasons, auxiliary units normally served away from their province of origin. The *Ulpia Traiana* in the name of the first unit is taken from Hadrian's predecessor, Trajan, whose full name was Marcus Ulpius Traianus, and presumably means that the unit distinguished itself in some way during that reign.

We now have a little more knowledge of the fort's anatomy thanks to a number of excavations in the castle area between the 1970s and the 1990s, although, as can been seen in the air photograph, the area available for excavation around the keep was so limited that

48   Newcastle. The bridges with the Roman fort area beyond, from the south

only a general idea of the fort plan could be established. The first fort on the site does not appear to have been built until the Antonine period, well after the Wall itself was driven through the area. It may also have been partially timber-built, with the whole stone fort constructed still later, towards the end of the second century. Whatever the case, parts of a substantial headquarters building have been found (extending beneath the medieval keep) and a granary, apparently in an irregular location, was discovered nearby. The north wall was found below the thirteenth-century Black Gate, but the precise location of the other defences will remain a mystery until further excavation is possible. As for the Wall itself, when last identified on the eastern side, it was aligned slightly to the north of the cathedral whilst, to the west, it is now buried below Westgate Road. Where it joined up to the fort is, however, uncertain.

More is known of the Roman bridge which stood approximately on the site of the present swing bridge (**48**, centre). It appears to have survived, much repaired and renovated, until the thirteenth century, although it is no longer thought that its medieval successors reused its piers. Two altars, dedicated to Oceanus and Neptune, were dredged from the river at this point (in 1875 and 1903 respectively) and probably derive from a shrine erected by the Sixth Legion. Many Roman coins have also been dredged up in its vicinity and were presumably thrown in as votive offerings to the river god. There are now signs of civilian activity on the south bank of the Tyne around the bridge and these may represent a detached part of the fort's *vicus*.

Rudchester (Latin name Vindobala), NX 112676

Thanks to the effects of the Industrial Revolution and the spread of Newcastle's suburbs (which, lamentably recently were allowed to cover the site of the fort of Benwell (NX 216647)), Rudchester, 13 miles to the west of Wallsend, is the first Wall fort to survive in a form that has never been built over. The air photograph (**49**) was taken from above the modern B 6318, which was laid out as a military road after the eighteenth century Jacobite risings. Between Newcastle and MC 34 (with a few exceptions) this road was built over and largely out of Hadrian's Wall, whose stone work was smashed up for hard core. This archaeological tragedy does at least have the advantage of making the Wall area highly accessible and, as it is extremely visible from the air, it can also make clear the Wall's relationship with other structures. This is rarely so true as at Rudchester. The road can clearly be seen to bisect the fort, which is itself visible as a playing card shaped platform (arrowed) in front of the modern farm buildings. This means that, like many of the other Wall forts (including the now vanished Benwell), the *praetentura* of this site (including three of its four main gates) extended beyond the Wall, possibly to allow more rapid deployment of troops ahead of the line. This design might be thought particularly suited

49   *Rudchester from the north-west.* © Crown Copyright/MOD

to a cavalry garrison, but as yet we do not know which unit was originally stationed on the site. Unusually, the fort has yet to produce a single garrison inscription and the only evidence we have is a mention of an infantry unit, *Coh I Frisiaunum* (from modern Holland), in the late fourth-century military list known as the Notitia Dignitatum.

When first described by Camden in 1599, the defences and some of the interior were still clearly defined but the construction of the Military Road through the site marked a period of extensive stone robbing for building purposes. The air photograph thus shows little in the way of internal detail. It also gives little clue to the extent of any external *vicus* settlement, although a temple to Mithras is known on the western side of the fort. The site sits only 75m to the east of T 13b, but this is no longer visible and even the line of the Vallum has been obliterated in the immediate vicinity of the fort.

Rudchester is set in a fertile landscape that has been heavily farmed for centuries, which has caused further damage to the site, as can be seen from the surviving traces of rigg and furrow cultivation within it. Farming here may, though, be very ancient indeed, for excavations inside the fort in 1972 produced a series of plough marks incised into the subsoil in the pre-Roman levels, showing agriculture in progress here even before the fort was built (Gillam et al. 1973, 84f). Similar evidence for late Iron Age farming has also emerged from Wallsend, Halton Chesters and Carrawburgh and establishes the presence of a pre-Roman arable landscape on a previously unsuspected scale. In this late prehistoric context, the siting of Rudchester may be explained by the line of an ancient route way down the nearby March Burn to a ford across the Tyne at Newburn.

Halton Chesters (Latin name Onnum), NY 99768

In the section westwards from Rudchester to Halton Chesters little trace of the actual Wall can now been seen, mostly again thanks to stone robbing and the construction of the eighteenth-century Military Road, although the course of the ditch and Vallum are clear over long stretches.

The fort at Halton Chesters (**colour plate 16**, arrow 1) lies just east of the point where the main Roman north-south road in the East, Dere Street (the modern A68), crossed the Wall at Portgate. This fort has also been heavily affected by late medieval and recent agriculture and it is now difficult to see on the ground. Nevertheless, the southern half of the site is still easily visible from the air, including an unusual third-century extension to the west, and even some internal detail can be made out in low light. Like Rudchester, however, the northern part of the fort projected beyond the Wall (again marked by the B 6318) into what is now known as 'Brunt-ha'penny field' (probably from Roman coin finds) and intensive cultivation has here almost totally destroyed the visible shape of the site.

South of the fort almost everything has been obscured by medieval strip cultivation, but faint shadow marks seen from the air from time to time had suggested the presence of an extensive *vicus* settlement, and this has now been confirmed and mapped in remarkable detail thanks to a recent large scale geophysical survey by Timescape (Taylor et al. 2000). The Vallum has also been obliterated in the vicinity of the fort, although it is known to have deviated to pass to its south. But the air photograph does show it coming back into view two fields further to the west (**colour plate 16**, arrow 2).

Two garrison units are known from the site. At some point in the second century the 1,000-strong, part mounted *Coh I Vardullorum Equitata* left an inscription at nearby MC 19 and so may have been based at the fort. In the third and fourth centuries both an inscription and the *Notitia Dignitatum* attest to the presence of the 500-strong cavalry *Ala I Pannoniorum Sabiniana*, from the Danube lands.

50   Dere Street just north of Hadrian's Wall from the south. DJW

One kilometre to the west of Halton Chesters nothing is now visible of the Portgate, which must have been the most important crossing of the Wall in the east in Roman times. The site lies at NY 987686 and is now marked by nothing more than a rather lost looking roundabout where the eighteenth-century Military Road crosses Dere Street. To the north of the Wall, however, the A68 shows its credentials as a classic Roman road, running perfectly straight for miles at a time. In the somewhat uneven terrain the full effect is often lost on the modern driver, who can only ever see as far as the top of the next rise (hence its alarmingly high accident rate), but from the air the road line can be spectacular. Figure **50** shows a long straight a few kilometres to the north of the frontier, followed by a sharp turn to the right and the beginning of another straight. It is also possible to see the way in which the modern road has drifted away from the Roman line in places. For example, at the point arrowed, Dere Street continued straight on, whilst the modern road can be seen to make a slight detour to the right before returning to the Roman line to the left of the wood behind the arrow.

Chesters (Latin name Cilurnum), NY 912702

Chesters fort, although a much visited display site, is considerably easier to understand from the air than on the ground. The whole area was emparked within the Chesters estate by Nathaniel Clayton after 1796 and the fort, which lay between the Georgian mansion and the River North Tyne, was landscaped almost out of existence. Fortunately his son, John Clayton, became interested both in the fort and the Wall as a whole and preserved the site from further destruction whilst conducting extensive excavations. The remains uncovered by his work (and that of his nephew, a second Nathaniel) are now conserved within a fenced-off area and accessible to the general public (**colour plate 17**). The aerial view shows much of the rampart circuit, with its angle and interval towers and five of its six gates. As with the last three forts, the site lay astride the Wall with three of the main gates projecting to the north. Short stubs of excavated Wall can be made out at the top and bottom of the picture, joining up to the southern guard towers of the main east and west gates. The interior follows a reasonably normal layout. In the central area the *principia* is clearly marked, with a well-preserved, vaulted underground strong room visible in its rear range (**colour plate 17**, arrowed). Slightly closer to the camera is part of the late *praetorium*, which has its own intricate bath suite, whilst lines of barracks can be seen to its right in the projecting *praetentura*.

We have already looked at the eastern abutment of the bridge that carried the Wall across the North Tyne (**colour plate 12**), but **colour plate 18** provides a much better view of the fort baths (arrowed) beside the river's west bank. These are amongst the best preserved baths in Roman Britain and formed the model for the Wallsend reconstruction. The colour plate also shows the line of the Wall between the river and the fort, surviving as a low ridge just beyond the baths, with the stone work itself only exposed for one short length.

There are records of no less than four possible auxiliary units in the fort at various times. The original Hadrianic garrison may have been *Ala Augusta Ob Virtutem Appellata*, which, as we have already seen, was subsequently stationed at Old Carlisle. Later, although probably still within the second century, the 1,000-strong part mounted *Coh I*

Vangionum left an inscription, whilst another inscription attests to the presence of a 500-strong infantry unit, *Coh I Dalmatarum* from the area of modern Yugoslavia. The best recorded garrison, however, was another cavalry regiment, *Ala II Asturum* from north-west Spain. This force began carving inscriptions on the site around AD 205 and was still present to be recorded by the *Notitia* at the end of the fourth century.

The presence of a large civilian *vicus* outside the south side of the fort has been known since Clayton's day, but its complex layout was little understood until Prof. J.K. St. Joseph began air reconnaissance in the 1950s. The drought of 1984 produced more detail and similar conditions continue to reveal traces of the irregular road system and strip buildings that made up the settlement. No one air photograph can show more than a fraction of the evidence now available, but composite plots of all the aerial data have been compiled, such as that drawn by the RCHME (Bidwell 1999, 116). The principal centre lies just to the south of the fort around an east-west road which forms a crossroads with the road leading from the fort's south gate. Indeed there is a possibility (as yet unconfirmed) that the east-west road projects down to the river, in which case it is not impossible that there was another bridge or ford at this point. There also seems to have been a small cemetery area behind the baths in the east and, despite many uncertainties, this detailed data now makes Chesters (along with Vindolanda and Old Carlisle) one of the best understood *vicus* layouts on the northern frontier. There is, without doubt, plenty more left to recover, however. For example, we have an inscription recording the presence of an aqueduct to the site, and it is to be hoped that in future geophysical work and, if possible, excavations will be conducted to supplement the aerial results.

One basic question still remains: the course of the Vallum around the south side of the fort. We have seen that it seems to fall in with the fort's own south ditch when approaching from the east, but its departure course to the west remains uncertain. There is evidence that the *vicus* might extend to the west of the fort, thus blocking the route and, if so, it is possible that the Vallum, in the fort's immediate vicinity, may have been totally obliterated at some point to make way for the civilian settlement.

Limestone Corner

Two and a half miles to the north-west of Chesters, the Wall reaches its northernmost point, at Limestone Corner on the summit of Teppermoor Hill. For the two Wall miles east of this point, on the long climb up to the summit, the eighteenth-century road deviates from the Wall line to run slightly to its south. This has allowed a wealth of archaeological detail to survive; we have seen part of the stretch in **47**. Most of the surviving features are quite subtle, however, often taking the form of robber trenches and other low earthworks and, as a result, they are generally far easier to appreciate from the air. For example, **colour plate 19** (arrow 1) shows the remains of MC 29 (NY 889711). Like others we shall see, the fortlet is visible not through surviving stonework, but by a robber trench which follows almost the whole of its original rampart circuit, leaving its shape literally etched into the ground. In front of it, the Wall ditch survives well, with its bottom holding water. The Wall line itself can be seen to either side of the milecastle as a rather fainter linear robber trench (arrow 2), whilst the Military Way (arrow 3) is visible rounding the back of the fortlet, terraced into a slope, and then continuing on to the west (right).

51   Limestone Corner from the east. DJW

As for Limestone Corner itself, **51** shows the line of the Wall here, again visible mostly as a robber trench. The same applies to the faint remains of MC 30 (arrow 1), which are now bisected by a field wall, and lie part way through a three stage course change executed by the Wall as it makes a westerly turn towards Carrawburgh. At the very northernmost point, directly in front of the milecastle, the ditch is noticeably shallower than usual. At this point attempts to complete it to its full depth were abandoned in the face of a particularly hard basalt. This is not to say that the Romans were physically unable to cut through the rock, for the Vallum ditch, which is visible emerging from a wood to the left of the modern road, continued straight through the area uninterrupted. Presumably the extra effort was simply not thought worthwhile on what is anyway a commanding position and, as we shall see, the Wall ditch was often omitted altogether in particularly strong parts of the central sector, whereas the Vallum never was. The result was to leave an active work face preserved in the ditch. But, although this fascinating relic is visible from the air as a rocky patch at the edge of the picture, a little beyond the milecastle, it is for once far easier to appreciate on the ground.

To the south of the Wall, the Vallum ramparts again show signs of the regular gaps cut when the Wall was abandoned during the Antonine Wall period, and behind it a small temporary camp is visible (**51**, arrow 2), with the faint remains of titulus type entrances. The Military Way can also be made out as it approaches the milecastle (arrow 3), before making a slight turn to the left and vanishing beneath the modern B road.

Carrawburgh (Latin name Brocolita*), NY 859712*

The fort of Carrawburgh lies in one of the wildest sections of Hadrian's Wall, three and a half miles west of Chesters, on moorland overlooking the valley of the Newbrough Burn. Little excavation has taken place on the site, but the air photograph (**colour plate 20**) shows that the whole of the relatively well preserved 3.5 acre fort lies to the south of the Wall line, which is again here represented by the B 6318. There have been excavations of the fort's headquarters buildings, but most of the excavated discoveries on the site relate to the external *vicus*. It is known, however, that Carrawburgh was a late insertion into the Wall system (possibly shortly before AD 133) because the fort was superimposed on the line of the Vallum, which had to be filled in to make way for it. The external discoveries comprise the bath house, a well shrine to the water goddess Coventina, and a Mithraeum, or temple of Mithras, which is visible as a set of rectangular foundations to the south of (behind) the fort itself. The Mithraeum is the best studied of its kind in the north and shows a complex development across a century following its construction shortly after AD 205, whilst the sacred well was of particular interest for the many thousands of coins left as votive offerings to the deity. Little more is known of the *vicus* from surface work, but air photographs suggest that it may extend both to the south and west of the fort. **Colour plate 20**, for example, shows what seem to be the robber trenches of a series of rectangular structures (arrow 1) on either side of the Military Way as it leaves the fort's west gate, and the ground appears to have been artificially terraced in their vicinity. There are also more signs of buildings in the top centre of the picture (arrow 2), a little beyond the Mithraeum.

As at Chesters, there are records of four different auxiliary units from the fort. The Hadrianic garrison may have been a 1,000-strong infantry unit, *Coh I Tungrorum*, which had earlier been at Vindolanda. But as the fort is rather small for a cohort of this size, it may not have been present in full strength. There are also inscriptions left by the 500-strong infantry cohorts, *Coh I Ulpia Traiana Cugenorum* and *Coh I Frisauonum*, which we have already seen as the later garrisons of Newcastle and Rudchester respectively. Yet as these are dedications to Coventina, they need not necessarily indicate that the units were actually in garrison. From at least 205 onwards, however, the garrison changed to a part mounted force, the 500-strong *Coh I Batavorum*, from the Rhine delta, and this unit remained at the site for the next 200 years, to be recorded at the end of the fourth century by the *Notitia*.

Two miles to the west of Carrawburgh, close to T 33b, the B 6318 swings off well to the south of the Vallum and leaves the Wall unencumbered to climb up onto the volcanic ridges of the Whin Sill. The next 12 miles are the best preserved on the line. But although the Wall is often fully visible to the observer on the ground, the aerial perspective still has its advantages. We have already seen T 35a (**colour plate 11**), but its neighbour MC 35 is a spectacular site from the air. **Colour plate 21** shows it lying right at the top of a line of sheer cliffs, which actually continue down a good deal further out of shot. The Military Way shows up well passing to its south (arrowed) and its two internal barracks can be seen. The site does, however, have one major anomaly, which can also be seen in the picture. As already mentioned, the milecastles are, in effect, fortified passages through the line and so normally have gates through both their north and south walls. When MC 35 was excavated however (Haigh & Savage 1984), it was found that although the site had the normal south gate its northern frontage was blank. Hadrian's Wall passed across it uninterrupted with little sign that a gate had even been planned. In many ways, this is hardly surprising. The cliffs to its immediate north mean that anyone passing through a gate here would be faced with at least a 50ft vertical drop, but if a gate would have been pointless, it does rather beg the question of why the Romans bothered with a milecastle at all. If the fortlet could not provide access through the line, its observation function could have been fulfilled equally well by a mere turret. It is, of course, possible that the Roman army simply considered themselves 'not paid to think'. In other words, it was time for a milecastle, so they built one and let someone else worry about whether or not it was usable. But the fact that the installation continued to be manned should perhaps make us wonder if it may be telling us rather more about what other functions these fortlets could have had, which did not require a passage through the Wall. Indeed, this is especially true if other milecastles were similarly cut off by the removal of their causeways across the Wall ditch, yet remained in use. They might, for example, have acted as garrison centres for the turrets on either side and this in turn opens questions as to how the line itself was manned. Most of the line installations were within easy walking distance of a fort, especially once the Wall forts had been built. This means that if their crews were simply small groups seconded from the nearest fort they could easily have returned home at the end of their duty shift and the milecastles should not have needed barracks at all. There is no real evidence either way, but it is thus tempting to wonder whether the line might have been held by some special force of its own. There is indeed documentary proof from Egypt that minor frontier installations, such as watchtowers, could be manned by civilians (Alston 1995, 87). This would seem improbable on a system as remote as Hadrian's Wall, but the whole issue of the organisation of the line watch may be ripe for re-examination.

Housesteads (Latin name probably Vercovicum*), NY 790688*

Housesteads is probably the best known of all the forts on Hadrian's Wall and, like Carrawburgh, five miles to the east, it lies wholly behind the line, although unlike its neighbour it lies long axis on to the Wall. The reason for this is the topography, since the presence of a rocky scarp made it impossible to project any part of the fort north of the Wall, whilst a steepening slope restricted the usable area to the south. The 5.5 acre interior of the site represents one of the best preserved and most completely displayed plans of a Roman fort currently available in Britain. The visible structures comprise the normal main range with the central *principia* (**colour plate 22**, 1), what is probably the best preserved commanding officer's house on the Wall (2) and two granaries (3) which still show the loading steps leading down to the fort's main street. There are also less common features, including a large courtyard building, behind the headquarters, which is thought to be a hospital block (4) and a superbly preserved flushable latrine (5) in the fort's south-east corner which gives a fascinating insight into Roman sanitary arrangements. In the north-eastern quadrant, rows of late barrack blocks can be seen. These are of the chalet type already encountered at Wallsend, and **colour plate 23** (1) clearly shows the gaps between the individual *contubernia* buildings. Like all of the Wall forts, Housesteads was added to the line after construction of the original design had been started and the fort overlies the levelled remains of a length of the Wall which included a pre-existing turret

(T 34b) that had to be demolished to make room for it. The remains of the turret have now been excavated, however and can be seen on **colour plate 23** (arrow 2).

Outside the fort, quite a number of features are visible and form patterns which are best appreciated from the air. A stone structure projecting from one of the south gate towers (**colour plate 22**) is medieval, but the foundations of five rectangular buildings can be seen behind the fort and these represent the remains of shops, houses and taverns which formed part of an extensive *vicus*, much of which was built over the filled in Vallum. Other buildings have been excavated but not displayed and to judge from a considerable assortment of undulations in the ground, visible from the air to the south and east of the fort, there are plenty more still to be found. Elsewhere, the remains of a bath house and temples of Mithras and Mars Thincsus have been investigated at various times in the valleys further to the south and east, and a large flat area several hundred metres to the south-east of the fort may be the remains of a parade ground.

Colour plate 23 also shows a range of agricultural features which are thought to relate to the Roman occupation. The Military Way is visible emerging from the fort's west (right) gate and a series of rectangular features can be seen fronting onto it on either side, which seem to be small fields or paddocks. Meanwhile, to the south of the *vicus*, it is possible to make out part of an extensive series of terraces that have been cut into the hillside to provide flat farming land in a style reminiscent of Inca or paddy field cultivation. The terraces might have originated in the late Roman period when some would say that the frontier garrisons may have become little more than soldier farmers and the forts might be regarded as largely self-supporting strong points. It must be said,

52   Housesteads and the Knag Burn gate from the south-east. DJW

however, that there is still a great deal we do not understand about the organisation and professionalism of the late Roman army and it remains perfectly possible that these fields and terraces were farmed wholly by civilians. Moreover, if the military did have a hand in their construction, it would hardly be the only time that an army has taken practical steps to foster its own supply situation. Certainly, however, the tendency of the late Roman army to include new unit types, which were frequently recruited outside the Empire (and are often, perhaps unfairly, described as irregulars), can be seen in the garrison lists for the fort. We do not as yet know the names of the second-century garrisons. But from the early third century onwards both inscriptions and the *Notitia* attest to the presence of *Coh I Tungrorum*. This was a 1,000-strong infantry unit for which the above average, 5.5 acre, size of the fort was well suited. It is possible that it was present at the fort still earlier if the records just mentioned from Carrawburgh actually reflect activity by a neighbouring force. Whatever the case, the cohort was joined at some point during the third century by two of the new style units, both of which were Germanic in origin. These were the *Numerus Hnaudifridi* and a cavalry formation, the *Cuneus Frisiorum*, although it has been proposed that these were in fact two different names for the same unit (Crow, in Bidwell 1999, 125). Interestingly, Frisian pottery types begin to appear in the *vicus* area at about the time these units arrived (Jobey 1979, 136ff) and it has been suggested that the newcomers may have been housed outside the fort itself, possibly in a series of small and rather rough and ready buildings (excavated, but no longer on display on the site) which are not too dissimilar to chalet style *contubernia* (Crow 1995, 72f).

53   Milecastle 38 from the south. DJW

Finally, the location of the fort along the edge of a low cliff (part of the Whin Sill) meant that it was difficult for traffic to approach its northern gate. Accordingly, a completely new passage through the Wall was eventually constructed at the easiest crossing point, on much lower ground beside the Knag Burn, just to the east of the fort (**colour plate 23**, arrow 3 and **52**). This structure is identical in design to a normal (single carriageway) fort gate, with two guard towers flanking the gateway itself, and it is probably best interpreted as a control point for north-south traffic; a role that would have been fulfilled by the fort itself had it lain on more amenable terrain. Just outside the Knag Burn gate a hollow area (**52**, arrowed) was once believed, by some, to be the remains of a small amphitheatre, but this is no longer thought to be the case.

Between Housesteads and the next fort to the west, Great Chesters, are three of the best known and best preserved milecastles on the entire line. We have already seen MC 42 (**43**), but MCs 37 and 39 (**colour plates 24 & 25**) are even more informative, especially as both have recently been re-excavated. MC 37 (NY 784687) lies on a cliff top, one turret spacing to the west of Housesteads, and contains a single barrack building on its eastern side. It differs from the last cliff top milecastle, MC 35, in that it does have a north gate. Indeed during recent work by J.G. Crow a number of its stone voussoirs were found and put back into position. The location of MC 37 is subtly different, however. As the air photograph makes clear, the fortlet has been skilfully sited at a point where the sheer cliffs break up just enough that it is possible to scramble up to and down from it on foot, and so the gate was of real benefit.

54   Milecastle 40 from the north. DJW

Colour plate 24 also shows two other features. Firstly, the Military Way is often superbly preserved in this sector and can be seen behind the milecastle (arrowed), still in use as a modern farm track. Secondly, the Wall ditch is conspicuous by its absence. As already mentioned, this is a common occurrence on these cliff top sectors, where the rock face itself offered more than adequate protection. Even here, however, the Romans showed tenacious attention to detail. The cliff line is broken by a number of small gaps and in each one the ditch cuts back in, sometimes for just a matter of metres, often through exceptionally hard volcanic rock.

Two miles further to the west, one such gap came to be occupied by MC 39 (NY 761678) and is now named after it: Castle Nick (**colour plate 25**). The site is broadly similar to MC 37, although its position makes it far more accessible, but it differs in having two internal buildings, rather than one. The photograph also shows the way in which the Wall continued to be used by later ages, for the series of stone structures attached to the back of the barrier on the hill to the east of the fortlet (arrowed) appear to be medieval shielings. Individual milecastle histories can be complex and excavations were able to show that the internal structures and gateways of both MCs 37 and 39 had undergone a series of changes from the second to the fourth century.

MCs 37, 39 and 42 are all easy to appreciate on the ground. Moreover, the last two are overlooked by higher ground in their immediate vicinity so that even the surface observer can obtain what amounts to a low level aerial view. Time has not dealt so kindly with the other fortlets on this sector, and although just about discernible on the ground, they are much better seen from the air. Figures **53** and **54** (both arrowed) show the remains of

55 The Peel Gap tower from the north-east. DJW

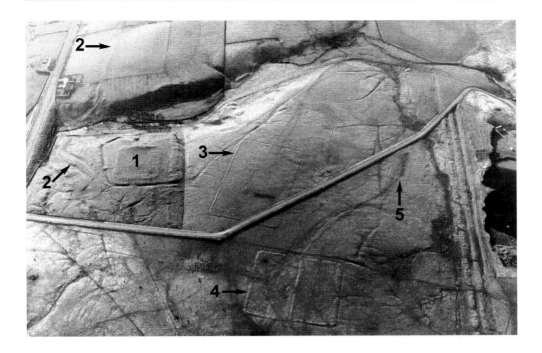

56   Haltwhistle common from the east

57   Cawfields from the north

MCs 38 and 40 (NY 773682 & 745676) which are again visible primarily as robber trenches; although not illustrated here, the state of MC 41 is similar.

This sector has also produced one complete surprise in recent years that is as yet unprecedented anywhere else on the line: a third turret at Peel Gap (NY 753676), on the Wall mile between MCs 39 and 40. The site was discovered by J.G. Crow during excavations on and around this much walked part of the line and, as can be seen from **55**, the tower (centre) watches a conspicuous pass through the Wall line between Peel Crags and Winshields Hill. The picture also shows one of the best engineered sections of the Military Way. It passes to the south of the tower (arrowed) on an embankment, before running into a cutting, out of shot, as it climbs up onto Peel Crags. It thus considerably reduces the (at times near vertical) gradient up which the Wall itself climbs.

In addition to the remains of the Wall itself, the area between Housesteads and Great Chesters is particularly rich in two other types of monument, both of which are best seen from the air. The first is the Roman temporary camp. One of the largest concentrations

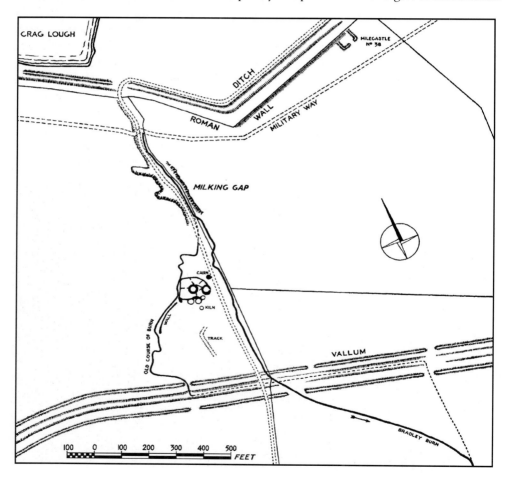

58   Map of the Milking Gap settlement and its surroundings. Drawn by H.E. Kilbride-Jones

of these lies around the Stanegate fortlet of Haltwhistle Burn, although they seem more likely to date from the Wall period. Figure **56** shows the fortlet (1), with the Stanegate road crossing the Burn to its south (arrow 2), and three camps are visible to the right (north) in the area immediately south of Hadrian's Wall's Vallum (arrows 3-5). Two of these camps are quite large, although one (arrow 4) has been divided in two at some point, and they may have been used to house the soldiers building the Wall through this area. But one (arrow 5) is extremely small, hardly larger than a milecastle, and it may be the result of a training exercise. These camps all lie to the south of the Wall and there are others in the area which space does not allow us to illustrate, but the camps also extend north of the line. For example, **57** (arrow 1) shows Cawfields camp and part of its larger neighbour Burnhead (arrow 2). These lie just north of MC 42, which is visible in the middle ground, with the Vallum and one of the larger Haltwhistle Common camps (arrow 3) in the distance.

The other common feature in this sector is signs of native activity and the best known site in the area is the farmstead of Milking Gap, just to the south-west of MC 38 (NY 772678). The site is visible on the ground, but it is far easier to understand from above (**colour plate 26**, arrowed) from where it shows as a series of circular structures and compounds. One of the most interesting facets of the site for of the Wall scholar is the fact that it lies in the supposed military zone between the Wall itself and the Vallum (**58**); this has led to much speculation as to whether it can have been occupied at the same time as the Wall. Pottery from the 1930s excavations was initially interpreted as Antonine (Kilbride-Jones, 1938), suggesting that the farmstead was established whilst the Antonine Wall was the active frontier, but a recent re-examination of the material would date it to the Trajanic period before the Wall was built. The most honest answer is probably that we

59   *Possible native sites on Winshields, with the Vallum bottom left, from the south-east*

cannot be sure, which is a pity since the answer might well shed light on the purpose of the Vallum and on the Roman frontier army's official attitude to the local indigenous population. Whatever the case, there are numerous other possible native sites between the Wall and the Vallum in this area, most of which have been located by aerial photography. The largest concentration seen by ourselves lies on the southern face of Winshields Hill, the highest ground on the entire Wall line, and **59** shows just a small selection of the total (arrowed). It should be stressed that none of these sites has been excavated and their dating remains completely unknown. Indeed some of the features could be almost anything from Iron Age round houses to modern cattle feeding platforms, but their sheer number is impressive and it is to be hoped that in time they will be investigated further.

Great Chesters fort (Latin name Aesica*), NY 704668*

Six miles to the west of Housesteads lies the next Wall fort, Great Chesters, which, like Housesteads and Carrawburgh, is attached to the rear of the Wall rather than projecting beyond it. Again like Carrawburgh, it appears to be a slightly later addition to the Wall fort series and, in common with several other Wall forts, its construction necessitated the obliteration of an existing line installation, in this case MC 43.

The site is famous for an enamel brooch found in the south gate in 1894, but the fort is little visited today, even though the south and west gates are visible along with a superb vaulted underground strong room from the *principia*, similar to that at Chesters. This is a shame but it is certainly true that it is easier to appreciate the fort fully from the air. **Colour plate 27** shows the entire defensive circuit, except for the north-east corner where the site has been overlain by modern farm buildings. To the west (right) of the fort

60   The Great Chesters aqueduct from the south

61   *A newly discovered temporary camp at Great Chesters, from the north-east*

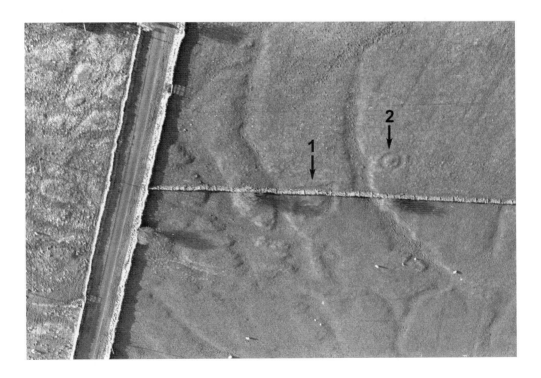

62   *Roman style tombs near Great Chesters, from the south*

an impressive set of multiple ditches can be made out, whilst to the south-east an area of terraced ground is visible (3), which might represent platforms for *vicus* buildings. In the interior, the strong room already mentioned can be seen in the fort's centre (1), but perhaps more importantly a group of late chalet style barracks can be seen in the south-west quadrant (2). These were once displayed on the surface but, although they have recently been reburied to protect them from damage by livestock, they remain fully visible from the air.

In many ways, however, the fort itself is of less interest, from an aerial archaeologist's point of view, than the features that lie around it, some of which are intimately connected with the site's life and operation. One example is the fort's water supply, which was brought in by means of a remarkable five mile long aqueduct, much of which can still be made out from the air and even, on occasions, on the ground. It follows a beautifully engineered contoured course through rough country to give it a gentle and constant fall. It also lay wholly to the north of the Wall, which could be seen as something of a risk given the harm that could be caused if an enemy was able to cut or pollute it. Presumably the Romans were confident enough of their control of territory well ahead of the frontier that they felt certain of keeping this vital piece of infrastructure safe. Figure **60** shows a well preserved stretch of the channel (arrowed) terraced into a valley side at the confluence of the Caw Burn and Pont Gallon Burn (NY 716677), about 2km to the north-east of Great Chesters. The entire length of the aqueduct is carried in a similar open leet and has none of the tunnels, bridges or inverted syphon pipes associated with the more grandiose water supply lines of major cities such as Rome itself.

63   Milecastle 45 from the north. DJW

Great Chesters is also a focus for more Roman temporary camps and despite many years of study, aerial photography continues to find new ones. For example, **61** (arrow 1) shows a previously unknown camp to the north-east of the fort, close to the line of the aqueduct (NY 717672). Like the Cawfields examples seen in **57**, this small camp lies to the north of the Wall, whose ditch can be seen in the background (arrow 2). The buildings visible towards the top right-hand corner of the photograph belong to the farm of Great Chesters and the fort itself lies just out of shot.

Roman soldiers were men in the prime of life but, as in any pre-industrial society, death rates amongst the Wall garrisons would have been high, mostly due to natural causes such as infection, rather than through military action. As a result, all of the Wall forts would have had cemeteries but, although we have quite a number of Roman gravestones from the frontier, the tombs have rarely been visible on the ground. Great Chesters may be an exception, however, for a number of features have been found from the air which resemble Roman tombs of quite high status. Two of these are shown in **62**, lying close beside the Stanegate road, at Markham Cottage, almost 1km to the south of the fort (NY 708659). The two features strongly resemble a group of better preserved tombs which can still be seen along Dere Street as it approaches the outpost fort of High Rochester. They constitute what looks to be a square ditched enclosure (arrow 1), now bisected by a field wall, which may actually be the robber trench of a stone monument, along with a circular feature (arrow 2) which again shows signs of stone robbing. It was normal practice to locate Roman cemeteries alongside roads. Nevertheless, this particular site may have another interesting aspect for there is a considerable native barrow field just a few hundred metres further to the west which looks from the air to be of Iron Age or even older date.

64   Turret 48b from the south. DJW

It is possible, therefore, that this area was already a cemetery when the Romans arrived and that the army simply continued using it.

Finally, three auxiliary units have been associated with Great Chesters, although one, *Coh VI Nerviorum* may not have been in occupation. The later second-century garrison seems to have been a 500-strong infantry unit, *Coh VI Raetorum* from the area of southern Germany, whilst from at least AD 225 until the end of the fourth century, the fort was held by a part mounted unit, the 500 strong *Coh II Asturum*, from Spain.

We have already dealt with the next fort, three miles to the west at Carvoran, whilst discussing the Stanegate. In the interim, however, both MCs 44 and 45 (**63**, arrowed) can be seen from the air by their robber trenches, as can MC 46 to the immediate north of Carvoran itself (**18**, arrow 6). From Carvoran, the Wall runs down towards its crossing of the Irthing at Willowford. We have already seen MC 48, the most complete milecastle currently on display on the frontier. But this site is just the start of a superbly preserved mile and a half long sector which stretches to a little way beyond the next Wall fort at Birdoswald. Its survival is all the more remarkable because the moorland of the central sector has now changed to lusher country, which has long been intensively farmed. Yet almost the entire length of the Wall can be seen in this area, except for a few short stretches where it is crossed by modern roads or railways, and three turrets (T's 48a & b and T 49b), another milecastle (MC 49) and the Willowford bridge are also well preserved.

Figure **64** (arrowed) shows T 48b surviving amongst the outbuildings of Willowford farm (NY 624665). T 48a, to the east, is essentially identical and in both cases it can be seen that the Wall immediately abutting the tower is slightly broader than the line as a whole. This is a feature of this area that is easier to see from the ground than from the air, but MC 48 shows the same phenomenon. The explanation seems to be that these installations were built first, with short wing walls so that they could be seamlessly integrated with the main Hadrian's Wall curtain when it arrived. These wings were built on the assumption that the Wall would be constructed to its initial 10ft gauge, and under normal circumstances they would have become invisible once bonded with the curtain. But by the time the Wall builders reached this sector they had reduced the width of the line to a narrower 8ft gauge. This was brought up to the northern part of each wing, to keep the outward facing side of the line flush, and so the wing walls remain detectable as short projections from the rear of the barrier.

The Irthing crossing itself is of great structural interest. Like the North Tyne at Chesters, the river has meandered a little way to the west since Roman times and the bridge now stands high and dry. **Colour plate 28** shows the Wall running down from T 48b towards the eastern abutment (NY 623665). This is now around 100m from the water, whilst the opposite bank has been steepened by erosion into the sharp ridge known as Harrow Scar, which is topped by Milecastle 49 (NY 620664).

Only some idea of the complexity of the abutment's history can be gained from the air. It was initially part of a bridge with stone piers and arches. This was damaged by flooding, probably between AD 150 and 175, and reconstruction saw a modified structure protected by relief sluices. Indications of timberwork at the top of the surviving stonework show that the replacement bridge was built predominantly of timber resting on stone piers, whilst to the immediate east a large tower (visible in the air photograph) was constructed. Around the end of the second century, the bridge was modified again to allow it to carry the Military Way. This involved the partial demolition of the tower to make way for a substantial earth ramp, which took the roadway up onto the bridge.

Both from the air and on the ground, milecastle 49 appears rather better preserved than it actually is. Although much of its original wall circuit can still be seen, the internal building visible in **colour plate 28** is a medieval insertion and not an original Roman barrack. The Wall itself is exceptionally well preserved west of the river, however, and on the ground a number of small inscriptions can be seen in its fabric, recording the construction of different lengths by a variety of legionary centuries.

Birdoswald (Latin name probably Banna), NY 616663

West of the river crossing, the Wall runs along the northern side of the Irthing gorge, and a third of a mile west of MC 49 (3.5 miles west of Carvoran) it reaches the fort of Birdoswald. The site replaced Nether Denton on the Stanegate and sits at the point where a road ran north to the outpost fort of Bewcastle. Its awesome setting on the edge of an almost sheer escarpment is best appreciated from the air, and **65** shows the fort (with MC 49 in the foreground) standing some 200ft above the river. The Wall itself can be seen running diagonally through the picture, across the northern front of the fort. But it should be remembered that we are now entering the area where the line was initially built of turf. The visible Stone Wall is therefore a replacement for the original Turf Wall. The vast bulk of the Turf Wall sector was replaced in stone on its original line but, unusually, over a two

65   Milecastle 49 with Birdoswald fort behind, from the north-east. DJW

mile front here the Stone Wall was run on a slightly more northerly course. When the fort was built, the Turf Wall was still in commission, and the site was originally set so that the Wall joined it at the southern gate towers of its main east and west gates. It would thus have projected beyond the Wall in the same manner as the forts from Benwell to Chesters. It was thus only later, with the building of the new stone line, that it came to lie wholly to the south of the Wall. As elsewhere on the line, however, the fort post-dates the initial building of the Wall and excavation has shown that a completed section of both the Turf Wall (which included T 49a) and its ditch had to be levelled to make way for it.

The fort and its environs have been the scene of substantial excavations both prior to the Second World War and more recently in 1980s and 90s, when the Central Excavation Unit of English Heritage excavated the granaries, the adjacent west gate and other structures in the north-western quadrant (Wilmott 1997). The granaries, as conserved after excavation, can be seen in **colour plate 29** in front of Birdoswald farmhouse, which itself incorporates a bastle or peel-house dating from the sixteenth century. Few other internal structures have been displayed, although virtually the entire defensive circuit is visible. But two large rectangular mounds which take up almost the whole of the space between the granaries and the east (right) gate mark the positions of the *principia* and *praetorium*. The fact that the backfilled Turf Wall ditch passed under the main range led to considerable subsidence in the southern granary (which was built surprisingly late under the Emperor Severus in AD 205-8). Nevertheless it remained in use and its subsequent development provides one of the most detailed stratigraphic sequences yet available from the final stages of a Wall fort's life. By the end of the fourth century the building's usage had changed in character from a military granary to a residential structure. It had apparently come to be occupied as a hall of some sort. After the collapse of its roof, this structure was rebuilt or repaired using timber uprights and it then seems to have been used well into the sub-Roman period. Exactly how long it survived still remains uncertain, but the building may help to shed light on the final fate of the Wall and its garrison. The popular imagination still tends to see the end of Roman Britain as an organised withdrawal, with the army sailing off to the continent in a last ditch effort to defend Rome and the imperial heartland. In fact the situation was considerably more chaotic and it is probable that all that really happened in a remote area like Hadrian's Wall is that the soldiers' pay eventually stopped coming. This would have left troops, who were probably by this time anyway recruited locally, to fend for themselves, and what these men would have done next has long been a question asked by Wall scholars. The answer at Birdoswald seems to be that some of them, at least, remained in the fort that had, after all, been the centre of their community for generations.

Excavation and air photography have long shown that a number of buildings and other structures (including a native promontory fort) once existed outside the fort. But these have now been unveiled in remarkable detail by geophysical prospection and shown to be far more extensive than had been suspected hitherto (Biggins et al. in Bidwell 1999, 157ff). At one time, the first author had speculated that the substantial *vicus* around nearby Nether Denton might have made the development of another at Birdoswald unnecessary. But this is no longer tenable for, as these new results prove, a substantial settlement did grow up around the fort.

66   *The western Turf Wall and Stone Wall junction from the west*

We do not, as yet, know the Hadrianic garrison of Birdoswald, but from AD 205, if not before, the fort was occupied by a 1,000-strong unit, *Coh I Aelia* (i.e. Hadrian's) *Dacorum*, from modern Romania. At almost 5.5 acres in size, the fort is big enough to have held such a large unit at full strength, and the cohort remained at Birdoswald until the end of the Roman period.

To the west of Birdoswald, the Turf and Stone Walls remain separate until just before MC 51. As a result, there are two sets of milecastles and turrets from T 49b onwards. These are generally differentiated by having TW (Turf Wall) or SW (Stone Wall) added to their nomenclature so that, for example, the Turf Wall version of MC 50 is designated MC 50 TW. This long deviation has provided a wonderful opportunity to study the Turf Wall in a rather more pristine state. But quite why the two lines should have remained separate over such an extended front has been the cause of much speculation. It was obviously unnecessary if the only objective was to move the line up to Birdoswald fort's north front and the explanation probably lies in the need for signal communications. Hadrian's Wall was originally laid out on the assumption that the main garrison units were to remain in the Stanegate forts to the south, and the milecastles and turrets were sited so that virtually every one had a direct view of a Stanegate installation. This allowed them to signal for assistance using the visual techniques of the day (Woolliscroft 2001, chapters 1 & 2), although it also caused considerable distortions of the official one-third of a Roman mile tower spacing interval. The Turf Wall here was thus set out so that its installations could signal south to Nether Denton and its accompanying tower at Mains Rigg. Indeed it was run along exactly the northernmost line from which such signalling would have been possible from the tops of the turret and milecastle gate towers. Unfortunately, when the new fort came to be built, it was unable to see part of this line, specifically the sector from MC 50 TW to T 50b TW. This relatively short blind stretch may initially have been seen as tolerable since the line installations involved would still have been able to communicate indirectly with the fort via relays. But the rebuilding of the line in stone may have been seen as an opportunity to rectify matters, for the new line was set out so as to be visible from the fort throughout. If so, it may not be a coincidence that the lines reunite at MC 51, which is exactly the point at which the original Turf Wall line comes back into visual contact with Birdoswald.

The Turf Wall itself survives patchily, whilst for a mile or two beyond T 49b SW the Stone line is again overlain by a modern minor road. But the two Wall ditches remain in excellent condition, as does the Vallum, and this 'Two Walls' area can be quite spectacular from the air. Figure **66** shows the western end of the sector with the Turf Wall ditch (arrow 1) meeting that of the Stone Wall (arrow 2) towards the bottom of the photograph, whilst the Vallum (arrow 3), which runs to the south of both lines, continues on. MC 51 lies just out of shot beyond the bottom right-hand corner of the picture (although it is visible from the air as a slight mound). But a segment of the Turf Wall superstructure can be made out (arrow 4) behind the narrow band of trees a few hundred meters prior to the junction.

Castlesteads (Latin name probably Camboglanna*), NY 512635*

Castlesteads is one of the least understood forts on the Wall, partly for the reasons evident in **67**. The replacement for the Stanegate site of Old Church Brampton, it lies puzzlingly detached from the line of the Wall. It does, though, occupy a similar position to its predecessor, in that it took advantage of a scarp overlooking, in this case, the River Cambeck (a tributary of the Irthing) from the south. Until the eighteenth century, the site was clearly visible (in a wood). But, with the establishment of Castlesteads House, almost the whole of the fort's internal area was landscaped to form the gardens visible in the air photograph. Nevertheless, its outline can still be traced on the ground (although the surrounding woodland makes it completely invisible from the air) and the nineteenth-century surveyor McLauchlan was able to make a beautifully produced and fairly accurate plan (**68**). Despite (or perhaps because of) this destruction, a substantial collection of inscriptions has been recovered from the site, most of which are still held under cover in a special structure within the gardens. Amongst other information, these show the presence at various stages of two different auxiliary garrisons, namely the 500-strong, part mounted fourth cohort of Gauls, at an uncertain date, and a 1,000-strong infantry unit, the second cohort of Tungri, in the third century. The latter may not have been present at full strength however since, at only 3.75 acres, the fort was probably too small to hold it.

Trial trenching in the 1930s (Richmond & Hodgson, 1934) provided more information and one discovery, in particular, suggests strongly that the history of the site is more complex than had been realised. For the excavations revealed the presence of an earlier turf and timber fort underlying the known stone site. This raises an intriguing possibility. It has usually been thought that this timber phase belongs with the Turf Wall, whilst the stone fort formed part of the general replacement of this part of the frontier in stone. It is possible, though, that this early phase belongs with the Stanegate; if so, this could parallel the situation at Carvoran where, as we have already seen, what may be another former Stanegate fort was retained in use as a Wall fort, but again left detached from the barrier. It should be stressed that this sequence cannot yet be proven at either site. Indeed such tantalising glimpses serve largely to show us just how little we know about these forts, a situation which will not improve until further excavations are possible.

67   Castlesteads fort site from the north

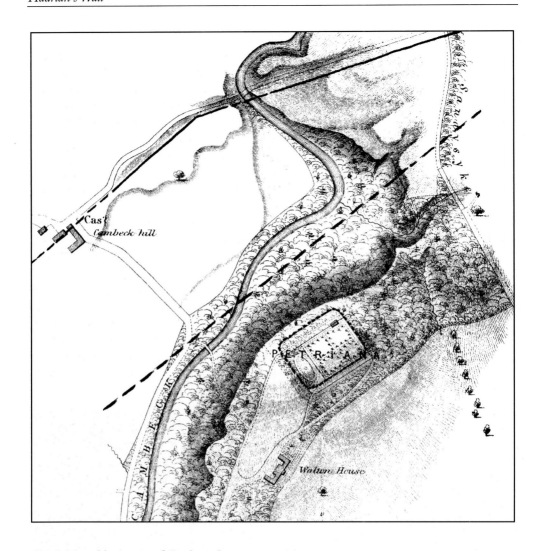

68   McLauchlan's map of Castlesteads

Fortunately, the same rather gloomy picture no longer applies to the fort's *vicus*. It has long been known that, unlike at Carvoran, the Vallum was routed quite some way to the south to include the fort. This takes it behind the Castlesteads gardens and across a gentle south facing slope which is now in agricultural use. Air photography had already shown signs of what appeared to be roads and buildings on this slope, but although this was enough to establish the existence of activity in the area, there was still little more to be said. The situation has recently been transformed, however, by a very large scale geophysical survey conducted by *Timescape*. This brought the scanty aerial evidence into far sharper focus by providing a detailed picture of a *vicus* to the south of the fort, beyond which lay field systems connected by lanes.

Stanwix (Latin name Petriana), NY 399571

Birdoswald is the last of the Wall forts where significant remains can be seen, even from the air, whilst Castlesteads is the last that has not been built over in post-Roman times. But even in the heart of modern cities, where no remains can be seen, air photography provides a way of showing the layout and topography of an ancient landscape that is both clearer and more immediate than a map. A good example of this is the next Wall fort, Stanwix, which lies almost eight miles to the west of Castlesteads.

With the coming of the Wall, Carlisle continued in use but the military focus switched north-east of the Eden to the present suburb of Stanwix, which is set on a plateau high above the river, some 1,200m from the castle. The site is relatively unexplored, but the fort is known to have been the single largest on the line (at over nine acres) and the base of the Wall's most prestigious unit. The fort's very name in Latin, *Petriana*, along with other evidence, attests to the presence here of the *Ala Petriana*, a member of the largest variety of Roman auxiliary cavalry regiment, an *ala milliaria*. These were elite units, nearly 1000-strong, of which only nine are known in the entire Roman world. The special nature of this garrison, whose commander would certainly have been the most senior officer on the Wall, has led to much speculation that Stanwix may have acted as the headquarters for some form of overall command for the frontier. But although this is perfectly plausible, it is certainly not inevitable and, for the moment, we do not have enough evidence to comment further. The whole issue of command is one that requires more evaluation, for if the frontier was to act as a single co-ordinated system, some form of unified command structure would certainly seem to have been desirable.

69   *Stanwix and Carlisle from the north*

Figure **69** shows the relationship between the two forts. Stanwix lay around the church in the bottom left-hand corner of the photograph, whilst Carlisle fort was at the position arrowed at the top right, where the medieval castle lies just out of sight. The Wall and Vallum crossed the cricket pitch, centre right, to a bridging point across the river, which again lies just out of shot.

In marked contrast to the Stanegate period, aerial archaeology has so far been able to make only a minor contribution to Wall studies to the west of Carlisle. It has enabled us to refine our knowledge of the exact course of the Wall and Vallum on occasions, and a number of new temporary camps have been found. But the main centres of interest, the three remaining forts of Burgh-by-Sands, Drumburgh and Bowness (**38**), have all long been built over by villages which cover both the forts themselves and the likely sites of their external *vici*.

Burgh II, the Wall fort of Burgh-by-Sands (Latin *Aballava*), lies around the church, towards the eastern end of the modern village (NY 328592), five and a half miles west of Stanwix (**32**). The fort itself has hardly been touched by archaeology, but what data there is suggests that it is a very late addition to the line, perhaps as late as the early third century. At the very least, it must have been built before AD 241, because the one garrison unit we know of from inscriptions on the site, the 1,000-strong *Coh I Nervana Germanorum*, had moved by that year to the fort of Papcastle. In 1980 and 1982, however, areas were excavated to the south of the fort in the rear garden of the former vicarage (partly in advance of the construction of a new vicarage). This located both curbs of the Military Way, as well as elements of *vicus* buildings fronting onto it. A full sequence, down to the natural subsoil, was established and as many as 17 distinct features were recorded,

70 *Bowness on Solway from the north-east*

including buildings and what may have been property divisions. The repeated rebuilding of these structures on roughly the same plots is of interest, as was the recovery of a great deal of slag and charcoal, indicative of metalworking. In addition it was found that a large dump of demolition material from a bath building had been used in the road makeup. As a result of these excavations it appears that the fort may have measured as much as 168-78m from north to south, which is larger than previously thought.

Recent geophysical work has suggested that, as at Birdoswald, the line of Hadrian's Wall was moved at Burgh, albeit probably over a much shorter front, to run up to the fort's north wall. The circumstances are somewhat different, however, and there are no signalling implications since both lines lay in full view of the fort. Instead, the Wall may have been moved when the fort was inserted so as to allow it to sit clear of an area of swampy ground (which once lay a little to the south) without projecting north of the line. Indeed, this configuration seems to have gone out of favour fairly quickly, since it was not adopted by any of the secondary Wall forts (nor by any of the forts on the Antonine Wall). There is evidence that the Turf Wall was replaced in stone much later in the far west than it was around Birdoswald: probably at some time in the mid- to late-second century, perhaps after the abandonment of the Antonine Wall. But it is unclear whether the fort was built as part of this wider remodelling or as a later independent project. Nor is it really clear why the fort should have been built at all after the line had managed without it for so long. The current assumption is that one of the other nearby forts, either Burgh I or III, had been the garrison centre for this sector until now. If this was the case, it might seem odd that any need should be felt to move this particular fort onto the Wall line when

71   Knockcross camp from the north

no such move was deemed necessary at other detached sites such as Carvoran and Castlesteads. It must be admitted however that not enough work has been done to prove this assumption either way, for we do not yet have a sufficiently detailed occupational history of either of the other Burgh forts. It thus remains possible that neither was occupied beyond the Stanegate period and, if this was the case, the new fort would have been a logical response to a potential weak spot, especially in view of the fact that, as mentioned, the Solway is fordable at this point. Indeed we would then need to ask why the fort was so long in coming.

Just over four miles to the west of Burgh, at NY 265598, lies one of the most mysterious forts on the Wall: Drumburgh (Latin *Congavata*). Only scanty excavations have taken place on the site, but they have been enough to show that the fort was abnormally small, at slightly under two acres. It has also been shown that, like Castlesteads, it had both turf and timber and stone building phases, with the stone fort being a little smaller still. The *Notitia* records its garrison as the 500-strong infantry cohort *I Lingonum*, but this cannot possibly have fitted into such a small space in full force. The fort lies wholly behind the Wall line, but nothing is now visible either on the ground or from the air.

The final fort on the Wall lies just under four miles to the west of Drumburgh, at Bowness on Solway (NY 223627). The fort, whose Latin name was *Maia* (big), was the second largest on the Wall, although recent excavations by Austen (1991) have shown that it was slightly smaller, at around 5.9 acres, than had previously been thought. Bowness does not appear in the *Notitia* and no garrison unit is named on inscriptions from the site. There are, though, two dedications by officers who call themselves 'Tribune of the cohort', one of which dates to 251-3, so the third-century garrison was an infantry or part mounted unit and, given the rank of the commanders and the size of the fort, a 1,000-strong force would seem likely.

Nothing of the original structure is now displayed on the site, but **70** shows the fort's approximate dimensions marked out by arrows, and its position on a scarp above the Solway estuary is clear. There is, though, one vestigial sign of the Roman occupation: the very straight main village street, which follows the course of the fort's *via praetoria*. Outside the built-up centre of the village, air photography comes back into its own and one discovery has been an unusual, irregularly shaped temporary camp, situated right on the waterfront at Knockcross (NY 230628). The camp (**71**, arrowed) lies several hundred metres to the north of the Wall, about 800m west of Bowness. It is tempting to see the camp as a fortified beachhead of some sort, perhaps connected with the supplying by sea of the Wall builders in this sector, but as yet no excavation has taken place on the site and its date and purpose are thus completely unknown.

4 The outposts and coastal defences

The Cumberland coast

Hadrian's Wall proper ran down to the Solway just west of Bowness but, with the Scottish coast still only a short boat trip away, its western flank was protected by a series of shore defences. There are forts stretching at least as far south as Ravenglass. But there was also provision for detailed surveillance, in the form of a chain of turf and timber milefortlets and stone towers which correspond exactly to the milecastle and turret system of the Wall. These reach at least as far south as Maryport (**72**) and are actually set at more precise one-third of a Roman mile intervals than the Wall installations. Indeed the only clear difference

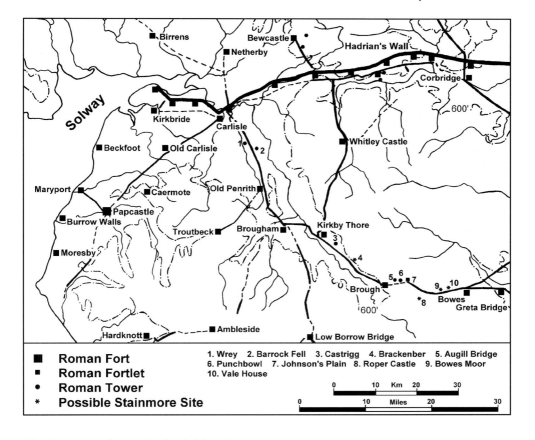

72 *Roman north-west England.* After Farrar

between these coastal sites and their Wall equivalents is that the milefortlets are surrounded by defensive ditches. In effect, then, the entire Wall system continued down the coast, except for the Vallum and the curtain wall itself. Since the 1970s, a combination of aerial photography and excavation has shown that these arrangements were rather more complex than had previously been thought and this is nowhere more true than on the first five miles of the system on the Cardurnock Peninsula (**73**). For example, **74** (arrow 1), taken in 1975, produced a clear image of milefortlet (MF) 1 at Biglands (NY 208619), but it also showed two running features (arrows 2 & 3) approaching the front and rear faces of the site from the direction of Bowness. These were initially assumed to be land drains or other modern features, but when trial excavations were conducted they proved to be small, Roman style, V-shaped ditches, 46m apart, 1.5-2m wide and 60-80 cm deep. The forward ditch had been re-cut twice during its active life, suggesting a reasonably prolonged period of use, whilst the rearward ditch produced a fragment of early- to mid-

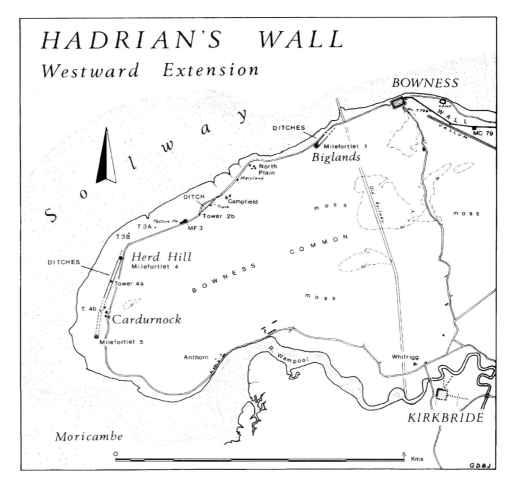

73   *The coastal defences on the Cardurnock Peninsula*

74   *Milefortlet 1 with running ditches, from the south-west*

second-century Roman pottery. In effect, therefore, the fortlet appeared to be located within a double-ditched cordon of primary construction (Jones, 1976 & 82).

A mile and two thirds further down the coast at Campfield (NY 191608) a photograph taken on the same flight (**75**) produced more surprises. This spot is the position of tower (TR) 2b and, as had been hoped, the site showed well thanks to a crop mark caused by the robber trenches of its foundations (arrow 1). That was not all though, for a few metres further to the west a second, fainter, square crop mark was visible (arrow 2), which appeared to be another tower. Furthermore both features were passed by a running crop mark (arrow 3) which seemed likely to be a ditch or, just possibly, a track. Subsequent excavation has now confirmed these indications by showing that at least one and possibly two earlier timber towers preceded the final stone tower, whilst the running feature was indeed a ditch. Moreover, an excavation by the first author, two miles further along the system at TR 4b (NY 171589), produced a similarly complex pattern, with a timber tower fronted by a palisade being replaced by a stone tower; unlike Hadrian's Turf Wall, there may thus have been a general evolution from timber to stone towers on this part of the line. There is currently however one slight problem with the data from TR 4b, in that the stone tower found might not be the Roman coastal installation, for its foundations differed from those seen elsewhere on the line. It is known that there was a series of revenue towers along this same coast to prevent smuggling in the eighteenth century. Indeed, one of them survives in excellent condition at Drumburgh, and it is possible that the excavation located another (Bellhouse 1989, 21f). Whatever the case, however, the important discovery is the

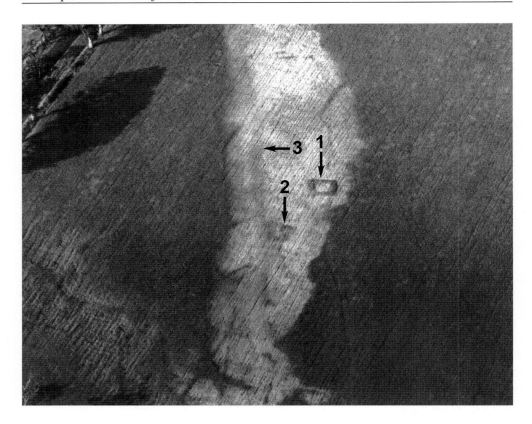

75   *Tower 2b from the south-west*

existence of the timber feature. For the real Roman stone tower must lie very close by and it is to be hoped that further work on the site can settle the matter more clearly.

The next drought, in 1985, revealed an extremely clear crop mark of the last fortlet on the peninsulaa: MF 5 at Cardurnock (NY 170585). The site lies overlooking Moricambe on the remains of a disused Second World War airfield, the construction of which was previously thought to have destroyed the site completely. A great deal was already known about the interior of this site. For rescue excavations, conducted during the war in advance of the building of the airfield (Simpson and Hodgson 1947), completely stripped the interior to reveal the remains of two barrack blocks. They also proved that the site had initially been rather larger than a normal milefortlet, although it had subsequently been reduced in size, and that it had had a somewhat interrupted history. The first usage extended from the Hadrianic period to the early third century, but there was then a break before occupation resumed in the fourth century.

The 1985 aerial evidence was most welcome in that it showed at least parts of the site had survived. But it also provided useful (largely external) data that had not been seen during the excavations. Figure **76** shows the fortlet (arrow 1) as a crop mark, which reveals the shape of the defensive ditch, along with a much narrower internal slot that may represent a palisade trench or a timber revetted frontage for its turf rampart. It also shows another section of the double-ditched cordon seen at MF 1, running away to the south from the fortlet (arrows 2 & 3), although this time the lines pass to one side of the site, rather than enclosing it as at Biglands. This and other photographs from the same flight allowed this feature to be traced for half a kilometre towards the foreshore, and subsequent excavations showed that the ditch system had an associated frontal palisade and internal roadway. If the cordon was continuous, as is yet to be proven, it could have formed a defended corridor along the whole length of the system so that, although (like the Stanegate in the west) the coastal system lacked the stone barrier of Hadrian's Wall, it still had a running barrier of sorts. The ditches seem to have been installed on the line in its very earliest days, but they might also have gone out of use fairly quickly, for the Cardurnock examples had been partly infilled by an iron-working deposit, dating to about 160.

Although forts and an occasional tower had been found to the south of Moricambe, the regular milefortlet and tower system was once thought to have ended at MF 5. But since the 1950s it has been traced for a further 17-18 miles to just south of Maryport. This has been almost exclusively thanks to the work of one extremely dedicated field worker, R.L. Bellhouse, but even here aerial reconnaissance has been of occasional assistance.

The first installation to the south of Moricambe is MF 9 (NY 130562), which stands on the Grune Peninsula, a narrow spit of land separating the sea from the channels and salt marshes of the estuary itself. The nomenclature of this site may seem curious but, in fact, milefortlets 6-8 do not exist. At one time it was thought that Moricambe was dry land

76   *Milefortlet 5 from the south-west*

in Roman times and Bellhouse originally allowed for a continuation of the system across its mouth when devising the system of site numbers. He himself (1962) soon exploded this myth however by showing that the inlet was much older than had previously been thought. This means that MF 9 should, strictly, be MF 6 and that all of the sites further south have been similarly misnumbered. Nevertheless, the established numbering system remains useful as a frame of common reference and it has been used for so long that it would only be confusing to change it now.

The field in which the fortlet stands is called Castlesteads and there had long been a dim awareness that a site of some sort was there to be found. But it was air photography by the late Prof. J.K. St.Joseph in the 1950s that established the site as part of the Roman coastal system. Figure **77** shows one of our own air photographs and the fortlet can be seen (partly overlain by a field boundary) as a rectangular parch mark (arrow 1) surrounded by the very faint dark crop mark of its ditch. MF 9 has not yet been subject to excavation, but its size can be gauged from air photographs and, like MF 5, it is noticeably larger than the rest of the milefortlet series. This discrepancy would have allowed both sites to hold slightly larger than average garrisons and it presumably marks their special status guarding the entrance to the estuary, as what amount to terminal fortlets for quasi-separate northern and southern sectors of the line,

Air photography has also revealed a number of other features at this site. The first, which lies two fields to the north of MF 9 (arrow 2), is a second, slightly smaller, rectangular ditched structure, resembling a more normally sized milefortlet. The second lies another field to the north (arrow 3), where two linear features (which resemble the

77 *Milefortlet 9 from the west*

double cordon ditches seen further north) can be seen heading into the estuary salt marshes. None of these crop marks has been excavated and so their identity remains uncertain. Bellhouse has informed the authors that he believes the running features to have been created by past wave action. The rectangular structure, on the other hand, could be virtually anything, especially as this area was used as a naval base during Edward I's Scottish wars and may well conceal defences dating from that period. Nevertheless this part of the peninsula would seem well worth keeping under observation and it is to be hoped that surface work, including excavation, will eventually take place.

To the south of Grune point, the next few miles of the system may have been lost to a mixture of coastal erosion and modern development. As a result, no more installations are known until MF 12, which lies just to the south of the seaside town of Silloth. Silloth itself was once thought to provide further evidence for a continuation of the northern cordon line. Figure **78** shows Silloth school playing fields (NY 113542) photographed in drought conditions in 1975. The grounds are based on sand and are extremely free draining. They thus show parch marks very easily and the photograph shows a number of features of both natural and artificial origin. Three of these appeared to be of particular significance: two dark and slightly converging lines (arrows 1 & 2), which resembled the ditches seen at MF 1, and a pale, curving line, with dark fringes, which seemed likely to be a road flanked by side ditches.

A very brief excavation was conducted on the straight features shortly after their discovery, which was only able to examine them in plan. This found that they consisted of dug slots that had been deliberately filled with a heavy clay that was not native to the site.

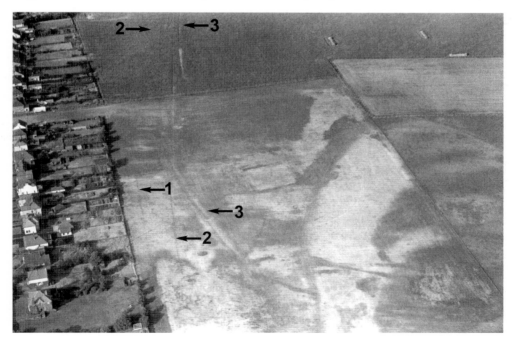

78   *Silloth playing field from the south*

This clay had loam inclusions, however, which looked very much like stake holes. It thus appeared possible that the clay had been laid to act as the foundation for a wooden fence of some sort and the entire complex was interpreted as a Roman road running along the coastal system (rather like the Wall's Military Way), fronted by a double palisade. Unfortunately, this proved to be illusory, for when more extensive excavations were undertaken by the writers in 1994, sections revealed that both of the straight features were modern pipe trenches. The road, on the other hand, which had not been looked at before, did prove to be real and, although no dating evidence was recovered, it had the structure of a Roman road and may well relate to the frontier.

Beckfoot (Latin probably Bibra*), NY 091489*

If Silloth has been something of a cautionary tale on the use of aerial photography, the next major site on the coast provides a superb demonstration of its potential. The fort of Beckfoot, although virtually invisible on the ground, is one of the most responsive crop mark sites in the entire frontier area. The three and a quarter acre fort sits just behind an open beach, on the theoretical position of TR 14b and was occupied at some, as yet undated, period by the 500-strong infantry *Coh II Pannoniorum*, from the Danube.

No one air photograph can do justice to the remarkably clear data now obtained for the site, since different weather and crop conditions mean that it shows different aspects of itself each year. Nevertheless, **79** provides a reasonable idea of what is possible. The fort

79   *Beckfoot fort from the west*

itself can be made out within a triple ditch system (arrow 1) and inside it the street grid appears as parch marks with the internal buildings visible in between. The *principia* makes up a clear dark square in the centre, with barracks behind it, whilst on either side of the *via principalis* just inside the south (right) gate are two rectangular buildings. Some air photographs show the latter so clearly that buttresses can be discerned which marks them out unmistakably as granaries (one obviously in an abnormal position). Other pictures have shown the foundations of the stone defensive walls in such detail that even the corner, gate and interval towers can be seen and it is, in fact, possible to draw up a virtually complete plan of the fort by combining air photographs. This goes a considerable way towards compensating for the near total lack of excavation carried out on the site to date.

The air photographic evidence does not stop at the fort itself, however. Both **79** and **80** (arrow 2) show a road approaching from the north, passing through the fort (arrow 1) and continuing on south. Indeed, **80** shows over a kilometre of this road. Whether this links up with the road seen in Silloth is not yet known, but there can be little doubt that the Beckfoot road is Roman and so there does definitely appear to have been a coastal equivalent of the Military Way, at least in this sector. Figure **79** also shows streets to the north (left) of the fort (arrow 3) which seem likely to belong to a *vicus*, and there are fainter traces of similar marks to the east of (behind) the fort. Other pictures have shown what appears to be a bath building inland of the fort, along with pits and ancient field systems to its south.

As yet, we are not sure whether the forts on the coastal system were slightly later additions, like the Wall forts, or part of the original plan. One problem on the coast was

80   Beckfoot and its surroundings from the west

81   Milefortlet 17 from the west

that there was no real equivalent to the Stanegate forts to provide a ready made backing to the frontier and, although the fortlets and towers would have provided intensive observation cover, they would have served little purpose by themselves. Again there is little point in having observers unless they can pass on word of danger to bases with the force necessary to do something about it. This would imply that forts were needed on this line from the start and that where they had not existed previously, they would have had to be built. There was of course one fort close to the line when it was built, the old terminal Stanegate fort at Kirkbride and, as we shall see below, Maryport might also have an early stage. But another of the Beckfoot aerial discoveries has sometimes been suggested as evidence for an early fort here. The feature is faintly visible in **80** (arrow 3) to the south of the known fort (arrow 1). The photograph shows parts of three sides of what is clearly a playing card shaped ditched enclosure, which certainly looks to be of Roman military design. The site is rather smaller than the known fort, at about two acres in area. Yet that already makes it larger than the Wall fort of Drumburgh and an interpretation as an early fort stage is perfectly plausible. Its ditch does appear rather narrow to be that of a permanent fort, however, and it is just as likely that the site represents a temporary camp. Indeed it may even be the construction camp from which the fort itself was built. Hopefully some excavation will be conducted here in the not too distant future to provide a clearer idea of its nature and date, and we still urgently need more dating evidence to provide a detailed history of the site as a whole. In particular, it would be useful to look for the remains of TR 14b (which has not been seen from the air) to see whether the fort was build over it, in the manner of several of the Wall forts, or instead of it, as part of a unified project. Incidentally, **80** is also a good example of the weakness of low wing aircraft as platforms for aerial photography. Although the picture was taken with the plane banked over to try to drop the wing out of the way, it is still very much in shot, obscuring the ground for some distance from the flight track.

Between Beckfoot and Maryport significant parts of the coastal system run at the edge of a series of cliffs which overlook sandy beaches and the sea. Parts of this line are, or have been, exposed to marine erosion since Roman times and a number of the installations had been thought to have been lost. In fact Bellhouse has been able to extract surprisingly intact archaeology from the most unpromising of environments in this area and things were already looking better than had been feared, but air photography was again able to play its part. For example, in 1977 MF 17, one of the most likely erosion victims, was photographed safe and well atop Dubmill Point (NY 079462). Figure **81** shows the fortlet's ditch (arrowed) clearly visible with the entrance break for its rear gate. There are even indications of internal structures, although the front gate is probably now buried beneath the modern road. Surprisingly, this site appeared well after the end of the normal crop mark season and was recorded through evening rain whilst returning from a flight mounted for a totally different purpose.

Another site which some had thought destroyed was MF 23, although Bellhouse had predicted a slight easterly kink in the line at this point, which would just about have allowed it to survive. This latter view was confirmed in 1979 when air photography finally located the fortlet (**82**, arrowed), again from the crop marks of its ditch, just a few metres to the south of the position that Bellhouse had predicted for it. The air photograph shows the site (NY 045380) bisected by a field boundary and again the rear (west) entrance break

82   Milefortlet 23 from the south-west

is visible. The north gate and parts of the ditch do seem to have been eroded away, but the interior shows something more of the amazing detail which air photography is sometimes able to reveal. The site has still not been excavated, but there is a line of five small black dots visible leading towards the cliff from the nearer side of the rear ditch entrance (and parallel to the side ditches). These almost certainly represent post holes and presumably belong to one of the fortlet's internal timber buildings.

Maryport (Latin name, Alauna), NY 038373

Maryport (along with Moresby) is one of the two exceptionally well-preserved fort sites of the Cumbrian coast. It stands on a high cliff, commanding extensive views in all directions, and overlooks the modern harbour town where, it has been speculated (so far without evidence), the Roman navy may have had a presence. The 6.5 acre site is almost square (**83**), quite unlike the playing card shape of the Wall forts. It does, however, strongly resemble the earlier Stanegate fort at Kirkbride so that, although the excavations conducted on the site to date have suggested a Hadrianic foundation, it is possible that the fort was founded a little before the building of the Wall. Not much in the way of internal structure is now visible, even from the air, for the site has suffered large-scale stone robbing, including the removal of a number of structures discovered in the eighteenth century (which seem to have included a rare internal bath block). Nevertheless extensive excavations in 1966 (Jarrett 1976) were able to show that the Hadrianic layout was sealed by later buildings (on differing alignments) of third- and fourth-century date.

83   Maryport fort from the north-east

Several hundred metres to the north of the fort, a remarkable group of dedicatory altars was discovered buried beside what might have been the parade ground. Similar parade grounds may have been a regular feature of most forts' immediate surroundings, although few have survived in recognisable form. There is, however, a superb example at Hardknott fort in the Lake District, and a flat area of ground to the south-east of Housesteads might be another. The alters themselves record the fort's late second-century garrison: the infantry cohort *I Baetasiorum*. Earlier, the Hadrianic garrison had been a part mounted force, *Coh I Hispanorum*, which had been replaced by the Antonine period with another infantry formation, *Coh I Dalmatarum*. The *Notitia*, though, records yet another infantry unit, *Coh III Nerviorum*, in garrison at the end of the Roman period. These units all have one rather curious aspect in common, for all were just 500 strong. Yet the fort is larger than any of the Hadrian's Wall forts except Stanwix and should have been more suited to a 1,000-strong force. This might be taken as supporting evidence for those who expect Maryport to have had a naval presence, for the sailors could have been co-brigaded with an auxiliary unit in a fort of this size. But for the moment we can only say that there is no evidence for this and the anomaly remains unexplained.

By the late nineteenth century various structures had come to light to the north of the fort, in the area between it and the supposed parade ground. These made it clear that there was a *vicus* in this area (Bellhouse 1992), but the scale of the settlement remained uncertain and aerial reconnaissance has, for once, been of relatively little help. A recent very large scale geophysical survey carried out by *Timescape* has, however, revealed a densely built-up area stretching for at least 200m to the north of the fort, mostly in the

84   Moresby fort from the south

form of a ribbon development along the Roman coast road, which was also traced. But there are more buildings and what appear to have been small fields behind this main street (unpublished, but plan available from the Senhouse Museum, Maryport).

To the south of Maryport, the milefortlet and tower system has only been traced for a further two miles to TR 26b at Rise How (NY 027347). There has been much speculation in the past that the logical place for it to have ended was at St Bee's Head, some 15 miles further south, where the English coast turns sharply away from Scotland. But years of searching by Bellhouse and others, both on the ground and through air photography, have failed to reveal a single additional installation and so it does now look likely that the system ended much sooner. That said, a tower seems an odd site with which to end the line and it is possible that there was at least one more milefortlet to act as a terminus. Indeed given the examples of MFs 5 and 9, as the termini around Moricambe, we could probably expect an unusually large site. Even if true, however, this may well never be proven, for the putative MF 27 would lie under the modern village of Flimby, where it is unlikely ever to be found.

Wherever the minor installations ended, three more forts are known on the line: at Burrow Walls (NY 004302), Moresby (NX 982209) and Ravenglass (SD 087958). All three show from the air to some degree, although Ravenglass is wooded and has been damaged by a railway cutting so that the visible area is small. Burrow Walls has surviving stone work but, of the three, the most impressive from the air is Moresby. The 3.5-acre site again occupies a cliff top with a magnificent field of view (except to the north where its line of sight is blocked by a headland). It partly underlies a churchyard and no internal structure can be seen, but almost the entire rampart circuit is still visible (**84**, arrowed). As

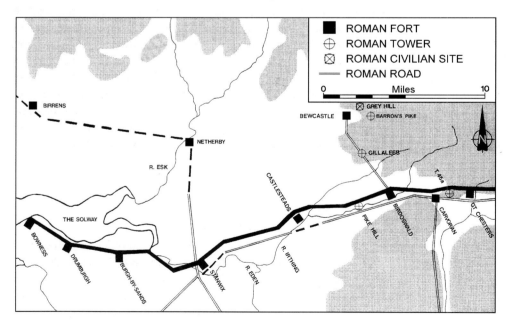

85   Hadrian's Wall: the western outpost system. DJW

with so many of the coastal forts, little excavation has been attempted and none using modern methods. Nevertheless enough inscriptions have been found to show its garrisons to have included two 500-strong part mounted units, *Coh II Lingonum*, followed by *Coh II Thracum* and, according to the *Notitia*, the fort's Latin name was probably Gabrosentum.

The outpost system

To the north of the Wall, the Roman army maintained a series of outpost forts. These were probably first and foremost intelligence gathering and early warning sites and most of them held 1,000-strong part mounted cohorts, which would have been excellent long range patrolling units. Many of the forts are also known to have held *Numeri Exploratorum*, or units of scouts, who may well have conducted more covert intelligence operations. Indeed, one fort, Netherby, was even called *Castra Exploratorum* (fort of the scouts) in Latin, which says something for the importance with which the presence of these units here was regarded. In the west, however, the outposts may have had a duel role as straightforward frontier forts, for there is a certain amount of evidence that the political border of the Empire stretched to the north of the Wall in this area. If so, this would help to explain why the western forts are arranged so differently to those in the east. The three western sites, Birrens, Netherby and Bewcastle, are deployed in a lateral east-west line (**85**), roughly parallel to the Wall, whilst the two eastern forts, Risingham and High Rochester, are set out in line ahead, as it were, along Dere Street (**86**).

Good communications are of obvious importance in an early warning system and all of the forts were linked back to the Wall by road. Bewcastle was also in signals contact with the Wall via two observation/relay towers at Barron's Pike and Gillalees Beacon (Woolliscroft 2001, chapter 3) and it would not be surprising to find similar tower systems connecting the other outposts to the Wall, and possibly also with each other. At one point, it was indeed thought that such a signalling station had been found at Four Laws (**86**) on Dere Street, a little to the south of Risingham. The site has since been proved to be post-Roman, but this does not reduce the likelihood of genuine sites eventually coming to light and air photography is undoubtedly the most probable method of finding them.

The sites

Risingham (Latin name Habitancum*), NY 891863*

To take the eastern sites first, the four acre fort of Risingham lies ten miles to the north of Hadrian's Wall on a plateau overlooking the River Rede. **Colour plate 30** shows the well-preserved fort platform, slightly eroded at its north-west corner and well protected by a multiple ditch system. In the relatively low light conditions a great many internal structures are visible, but these are not the original fort buildings. Instead they represent the remains of a now abandoned post-Roman settlement which used the fort as a quarry and as a ready made set of defences. Archaeology has proved, however, that the visible fort

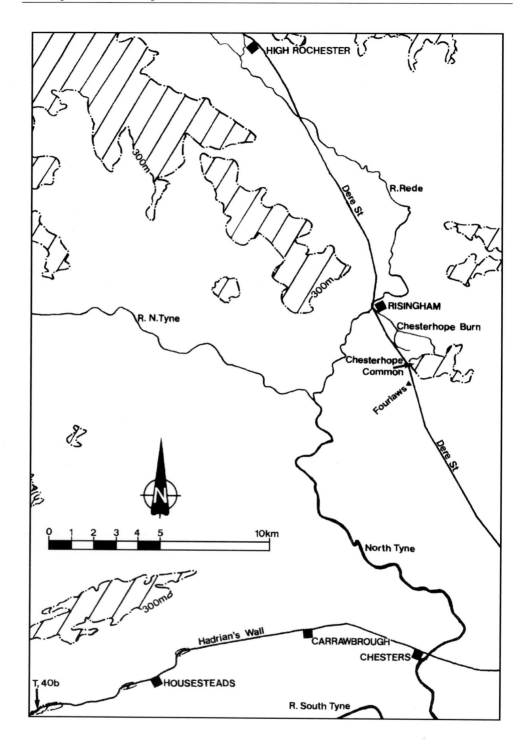

86   *Hadrian's Wall: the eastern outpost system.* DJW

is a late (third to fourth century) rebuild and the photograph shows a number of design differences between this site and the more classical Roman forts of the Wall itself. Firstly, the fort is only known to have two gates. These are clearly visible in its south (right) and west (far) sides, as are the causeways that provided access through the ditches. The situation in the damaged north front is slightly unclear and so a third gate may have been provided, but both the ditches and rampart can be seen to pass completely unbroken along the eastern (near) side. The south gate also shows a more defensive style of architecture, for two mounds are visible projecting from the entrance. These are the remains of projecting gate towers (instead of the flush towers of earlier forts) which would have allowed attacks on the gateway itself to be subjected to enfilading fire from the defenders. Refinements of this type are rare in northern Britain, but common elsewhere in the late Roman world. Early Roman forts were not really designed as heavily defensive structures, intended to withstand a siege. They were essentially armoured barracks for a self-confident army that preferred to fight in the open. But, by the end of the Roman occupation forts such as Pervensey, on the south coast, came much more to resemble medieval castles, with irregular shapes, heavily protected gates, and walls with frequent projecting bastions. Risingham would appear to be a small intermediate step in this progression. But it was still as far down this more defensive road as any of the forts in the stubbornly conservative Wall area was ever to go.

In origin, the fort may be an Antonine, rather than a Hadrianic, foundation and in the late second century the garrison was the 500-strong, part mounted cohort *IV Gallorum*. By the early third century, however, this had been moved to Vindolanda and been replaced by the 1,000-strong, part mounted *Coh I Vangionum*. None of the outposts remained in use until the time of the *Notitia*: they seem to have been abandoned in the first half of the fourth century. But the norm elsewhere in the Wall area was that third-century garrisons stayed at the same base into the fourth, and so this cohort probably remained at Risingham for the rest of the fort's service history. It was however supplemented, at some point, by a *Numerus Exploratorum* and a *Vexillatio Raetorum Gaesatorum* (a detachment of south German spearmen) and one wonders whether all of these units at full strength can have been fitted inside this relatively small fort.

As yet neither excavation nor air archaeology has detected signs of a *vicus* around the fort, but this may be due to the fact that this is pasture country which does not tend to produce crop marks. Certainly there is evidence for civilians, including children, from tombstones recovered from the site and it is probable than any settlement would have grown up along Dere Street as it passes to the west of the fort.

High Rochester (Latin name, Bremenium), NY 827988

The five-acre fort of High Rochester lies eight and a half miles north of Risingham on a high ridge overlooking Redesdale and the Sills Burn valley. The fort platform survives in clearly recognisable form (**87**) but it is now partly occupied by a farm and its outbuildings (themselves of some antiquity) which are mostly built of robbed Roman stone. Little internal detail can be seen today, even from the air, although the ditch system survives well. But excavations, largely in the 1850s, have provided evidence for chalet barracks and four, rather than the normal two, granaries. The fort shows no signs of the late Roman defensive refinements seen at Risingham, except that the west gate is slightly recessed. But a third-century inscription refers to a *ballistarium* or artillery platform, which suggests that resolute defensive measures were being taken. The fort has the normal four gates, but these are generally given only a single portal, rather than the double portals of the Wall fort gates, and this is probably an additional security precaution. Indeed it was also soon adopted on the Wall itself, where many of the Wall fort gates eventually had one or even both of their portals walled up.

The first occupation seems to have been in the late first century, during the Flavian occupation of Scotland, but the fort was then abandoned and only reoccupied, like Risingham, during the Antonine period. Inscriptions have shown that the Antonine garrison was the 500-strong part mounted cohort *I Lingonum*, which may have been replaced later in the second century by an infantry formation, *Coh I Dalmatarum* (or possibly *Dacorum*). The third, and probably early fourth-century garrison was much larger, however, (which may explain the extra granary capacity) and broadly similar to that at Risingham: the 1,000-strong part mounted *Coh I Vardullorum*, and a unit of scouts actually named after the fort, *Numerus Exploratorum Bremensium*.

As at Risingham, neither excavation nor air photography has revealed signs of a *vicus*, although the existence of women's tombstones may point to a civilian presence.

87 High Rochester fort from the north-east. Photo by T. Gates, copyright reserved

Recent work by Crow has revealed an area of industrial activity along Dere Street, to the east of the fort, but even this did not produce traces of a settlement (Crow in Bidwell 1999, 188ff).

For much of the Roman period High Rochester was the very northernmost outpost of imperial rule and its setting remains suitably atmospheric. The whole of the area to its north is now largely given over to a military training ground and its somewhat desolate appearance lends in the imagination something of the impression that the site might have given when it guarded the wild and exposed crossing of the Cheviot Hills from Tweedsdale. Remarkably, this same area may also have been used for training purposes in Roman times. A few miles further north along Dere Street are two large complexes of superimposed temporary camps: at Chew Green (NT 787085), which also had a more permanent fortlet, and Pennymuir (NT 754138). In between these two is the Iron Age hillfort of Wooden Law (NT 767125) which is invested by a series of Roman siege works built at a time when it does not seem to have been occupied. It would thus appear to have been adopted as a Roman training facility and, as we shall see below, there were similar arrangements close to the western outpost fort of Birrens.

Bewcastle (Latin name probably Fanum Cocidi*), NY 565746*

To turn now to the western outposts, Bewcastle lies six miles to the north of Birdoswald (**87**) on the Roman road known as the Maiden Way. The site stands on a small natural plateau of about six acres on the northern bank of the Kirkbeck, which has forced a distinctly non-standard shape on the fort itself. Every other Roman fort we have seen has been a quadrilateral with rounded corners (either a playing card shape or, more rarely, a square) and this is also the form adopted by almost every other Roman fort in the Empire. Bewcastle, however, is unique in having an irregular hexagonal ground plan and **colour plate 31** shows the way that this form has been adopted so as to fit the base into the limited space available. The outline of the fort can be made out reasonably clearly in the photograph, with the western (right) ditch and rampart defences particularly well preserved, to the left of a modern minor road. The north-east corner has been destroyed by a medieval castle (which is largely built of Roman stone) and parts of the interior now underlie Bewcastle churchyard (with its famous Anglo-Saxon cross) and the demesne farm. But, despite this disturbance, some internal detail, including parts of the *principia*, can be made out as slight bumps in the ground between the farm and the churchyard. Nevertheless, our principle knowledge comes from excavations carried out prior to the Second World War and, more recently, by Austen (1991a). These have shown something of the way in which the normal Roman fort buildings were fitted into the irregular layout (**88**) and have located an unusual, but substantial, internal bath house. They have also told us something of the history of the fort, which has Hadrianic, Severan, Diocletianic and Constantinian construction periods.

Only one garrison unit is currently known, a 1,000-strong infantry cohort, *I Aelia Dacorum*, which was present in the Antonine period in or around AD 145 and was later to move to Birdoswald. No third-century garrison is known with certainty, but a similar pattern to the other outposts with a 1,000-strong, part mounted unit, perhaps accompanied by a *Numerus Exploratorum*, would not be an unreasonable expectation.

At present no *vicus* is known, although indistinct air photographic features can be seen outside the ramparts to the west. But the second author has excavated a Roman style farm building on Grey Hill, about a mile to the north-east (NY 569761), which is presumably associated with the fort (Woolliscroft *et al.* 1989). We have already seen that the bath block is inside the fort, whereas one would normally expect to find it in the *vicus*, but we know from inscriptions of at least two temples, which may have lain outside. One of these was sacred to the native god Cocidius, who was obviously of some importance on the site. For not only do we have a considerable number of dedications to him, some of which were made by high ranking officers, but the Latin name *Fanum Cocidi* means temple of Cocidius.

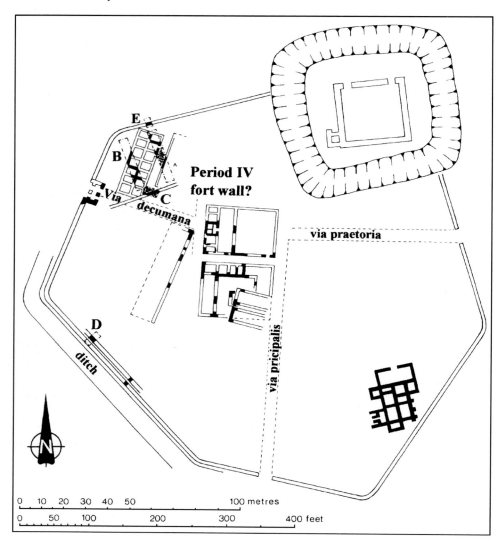

88   *Bewcastle fort, excavation plan.* Reproduced by kind permission of P.S. Austen

The view between Bewcastle and the Wall is blocked by a steep-sided but flat-topped hill called Gillalees Beacon and a Roman tower has long been known here, which must have formed part of a signalling link between the two (NY 579718). Unfortunately, although this site could see the Wall fort of Birdoswald, it was not in visual contact with Bewcastle and there is no point anywhere on the hill from which both forts can be seen simultaneously, even from the full height of a Roman tower. For many years this created something of a mystery but a second tower has now been located at Barron's Pike, one and three-quarters miles to the east of Bewcastle (NY 596752). This can link the fort to the Gillalees tower and thus we have a simple two stage relay system back to the Wall, with the added advantage that Barron's Pike is also directly intervisible with Carvoran. Neither tower photographs well at ground level, but as both lie within the airspace of RAF Spadeadam (a somewhat secretive establishment) they are difficult to photograph from the air. It is, though, possible to compromise and photograph the sites from the top of a telescopic 6m camera pole and **89** shows Barron's Pike pictured in this semi-aerial manner. The site is reminiscent of Mains Rigg on the Stanegate, with a defensive ditch (in this case circular, which is more normal) broken by a single entrance break. The site has not been excavated, except for a single section across its ditch, but the tower would have lain towards the centre, where the picture shows a human figure (actually a well known egyptologist) to provide a sense of scale.

The next outpost to the west is Netherby (NY 3971), one of the Wall's greatest archaeological mysteries. The site lies beside the River Esk, about nine miles to the north of Stanwix, and was reported as visible by early antiquaries. In 1732 a bath building was excavated, probably but (given Bewcastle's internal baths) not certainly from the *vicus*, and quite a number of inscriptions have come to light. In the later eighteenth century, however,

89   Barron's Pike tower, elevated view, from the south. DJW

the area was emparked and partly built over by Netherby Hall and the fort so thoroughly landscaped that even its exact location is no longer known. There is nothing now to see on the site, even from the air. Nevertheless, the inscriptions provide a reasonable amount of information. In particular, we know that the garrison in at least the early third century was yet another 1,000-strong part mounted unit, *Coh 1 Aelia Hispanorum*, and, as the fort's name is *Castra Exploratorum* (fort of the scouts), this was presumably accompanied by a *Numerus Exploratorum*. There is also, however, a later third-century inscription by another 1,000-strong part mounted unit, *Coh 1 Nervana Germanorum*, which is thought to come from the site. This unit (named after Hadrian's predecessor but one, Nerva) might just have replaced the Spaniards at some point in the century, but we have already seen that it was normal in the Wall area for early third-century garrisons to remain at the same fort for the remainder of its occupation. It is possible that something exceptional happened here, such as the Spanish unit being wiped out or disgraced. But it is also possible that the Germans are actually the missing garrison of Bewcastle; either the stone's provenance has become confused, or some members of the unit left an inscription whilst at Netherby on duty, for the inscription is a dedication to Cocidius who, as we have just seen, was particularly associated with Bewcastle.

Birrens (Latin name Blatobulgium), NY 218752

The last of the outpost forts was also the shortest lived, for Birrens seems to have been abandoned at some point after the return from the Antonine Wall, in the later second century whilst the remainder seem to have stayed in use until the early fourth century. It lies some nine miles to the west of Netherby on a bluff overlooking the Mein Water and measures approximately 4.9 acres. Two garrison units are known, both of which are yet again 1,000-strong part mounted cohorts. At some point before AD 158 there are records of *Coh I Nervana Germanorum* which, as we have just seen, may later have been moved to Bewcastle. After 158 the site became home to *Coh II Tungrorum*, which was later to be based at Castlesteads.

The site is clearly visible today with its impressive multiple ditch system and, under the right conditions, aerial photography can show much of its internal layout. **Colour plate 32**, for example, has caught the entire defensive circuit (except in the south where the site has been eroded by the stream) and a series of parch marks picks out almost the entire internal street grid, with the *principia* showing clearly in the centre. Air photographs also show another feature that is difficult to discern of the ground: a second large rectangular enclosure to the west (left) of the fort, which abuts onto the latter's western rampart, but otherwise has its own defences. This site also appears on **colour plate 32** as a series of parch marks, but its internal arrangements are less clear. There is a road heading west across the site from the fort's west gate, and two heading north, only one of which lies at a right angle to the east-west street. Nevertheless, the air photograph would suggest that all three pass out of the enclosure through two deliberate entranceways. Other structures can be made out dimly in the interior, but they do not make a recognisable pattern and, unlike the fort, which has been almost totally excavated in various stages since the end of the nineteenth century, no excavation has taken place here. The enclosure may form an unusually large and well-defended annex. It may be a walled *vicus* like that at Wallsend. It may be part of a much larger fort stage that was later reduced in size (in the manner of Vindolanda) or it may be a completely separate fort. There is even the possibility is that it is, in effect, a semi-detached fort. These are unknown, so far, in Britain, but in Roman Germany two units were occasionally brigaded on the same site in two forts sharing a party wall. A prime example is the fort of Osterburken on the *Limes* (pronounced Leemase), the German equivalent of Hadrian's Wall. Given Birrens' relatively small size and the fact that the outposts tended to have their large auxiliary cohorts brigaded together with scout units (albeit it is not as yet known if there was one here), this sort of arrangement would make sense, but we cannot know the true situation until more work has been done in this part of the site. It is interesting that the main Roman road to the north is now known to run from this enclosure, rather than from the fort, which suggests that the feature may be primary. A recent large scale geophysical survey by N.J. Lockett (with the second author present) was able to trace the route for some distance to the north of the site, whilst the road emerging from the fort's own north gate appeared to stop as soon as it had passed through the ditches. The same survey revealed a circular feature to the north of the enclosure which somewhat resembled a watchtower, and a fortlet has long been known from the air on a hill several hundred metres to the south. It is thus possible that the site was occupied in some way before the fort was built and/or after its early abandonment.

Three miles to the north-west of Birrens lies one of the most spectacular sites on the entire Hadrian's Wall complex. This is the Iron Age hillfort of Burnswark (NY 185787), a dramatic steep-sided, flat-topped hill with views which in some directions stretch for over 30 miles. The interest of the site for the Wall scholar rests not so much with the hilltop

90   Burnswark hillfort with its surrounding siege works, from the south-west

itself, as with a number of structures around its sides, for the site shows the most complete set of Roman siege works to have survived in Britain. Figure **90** shows the hill on a (sadly) slightly hazy day and the tumbled remains of the Iron Age rampart around the entire top of the hill can be made out without difficulty. Much more clearly visible, however, is a substantial Roman temporary camp to the south (right) of the hill (arrow 1) and part of a second camp to its north (arrow 2). The northern camp is relatively conventional, but the south camp has three large mounds projecting from its northern rampart towards the hillfort, which appear to have been artillery platforms built to carry the Roman army's powerful torsion-based stone throwing and arrow firing machines. Excavations in the nineteenth century also claimed to have found smaller camps and a complete circumvallation, or siege wall, around the hill, making this almost as elaborate a set of siege works as the famous site of Masada in Israel. Some of these details are now disputed, but there were still sure signs of a Roman attack, including stone catapult balls and numerous lead sling bullets that had been fired at the hillfort's main gate. Moreover the camps showed signs of careful construction and at least some internal stone buildings, as if a prolonged occupation was envisaged. Yet more recent excavations by Jobey (1977) have suggested that the Iron Age site was not occupied when attacked. The explanation may well be that this strong, but long abandoned, hillfort was used as a semi-permanent training centre by the Roman army, where the techniques of siegecraft and artillery firing could be practised. If so, it is interesting that here, as at Wooden Law, the training ground lay well to the north of the Wall. The date of this complex is uncertain, but the south camp's north-east corner overlies (and so post-dates) a small Antonine fortlet (arrow 3), which suggests that the army may already have fallen back from the Antonine Wall when it was using this area. If this is true, it speaks volumes for the self-confidence of the Roman military. It would in effect have been siting a major training facility on what was, at least theoretically, hostile territory.

5 Postscript

We began this book by saying that Hadrian's Wall was one of the most closely studied archaeological monuments on Earth, and so it is. But, from an aerial archaeologist's point of view, it can sometimes seem to be a victim of its own success. For a start, there has been rather less flying on the Wall than one might expect for so important a complex, possibly because so much is already known that air photography may have seemed to some to have little more to offer. Hopefully, this book will give the lie to that. There is a tremendous amount still to be achieved, particularly in fields such as the study of *vici*, the Cumberland coast, native activity and the Stanegate. Secondly, because so much is visible on the surface, archaeologists are perhaps less careful than they might be elsewhere in picking exactly the right time to fly so that crop, soil and/or shadow marks are likely to be at their best. One can fly over the Wall at any time of year and obtain useful photographs, but this is no reason to forget the normal disciplines of the aerial archaeologist's craft. Thirdly, the Wall itself has tended to act rather too much as a magnet to those who do practice air photography in the area. This is perfectly understandable. The line is such an awesome sight from the air that it is hard to break away from it. But this has led to a neglect of areas immediately surrounding it, whose own archaeology is vital if we are to understand the frontier in its wider context. This is so much the case that a recent aerial survey conducted for the Northumbria National Park (T. Gates, Pers comm) was able to record upstanding monuments within a short walk of the Wall which had never before been noticed. If such well-preserved sites have been missed, surely ploughed-out features that will only appear in special conditions as crop marks must have suffered even more neglect. Such problems affect our knowledge of the Roman presence, but still more they affect our understanding of contemporary native society. There have been major aerial surveys of areas both to the south and (at least as importantly) to the north of the line, by Jobey in the east and by the first author and N.J. Higham in the west, which have yielded a rich harvest of new sites. But there is a vast amount still to be done. Professional archaeologists will continue to fly over this ground and their timing and techniques will, hopefully improve. But the authors would like to make a special plea to private pilots, both in the Wall area and indeed all over the country, to carry cameras on their own flights. There are plenty of active private pilots who fly more hours per month than we can in a year. Moreover, they often fly regularly and can watch a crop mark develop, or judge likely lighting conditions, so as to capture a site when it is showing at its absolute best, when we may have caught it well short of its prime or, just as probably, missed it altogether. Aerial archaeology is one of the few areas left in science where the amateur can exceed the professional and it can make a fascinating additional hobby for both pilots and their passengers. This book will, we hope, provide aspiring air photographers with an idea of the sort of things to look out for, and more detailed books on technique are available (e.g. Wilson 2001). There are also a number of bodies who would be eager to see copies of any photographs, notably English Heritage, the Royal Commission on the Ancient and Historical Monuments of Scotland and Cadw in Wales, as well as, of course (for the Wall area and Roman Scotland), ourselves.

As for the future, individual air photographs of previously unknown sites will always have their own special value. But any long-term impact lies in their cumulative contribution to our overall knowledge of the past and their unique potential to assist in the understanding and management of the historical landscape. This needs a great deal of work in collating and assimilating large amounts of accumulated aerial data, which itself requires far freer access to that data by interested scholars and the public as a whole. In the past, this has been one of air photography's principle weak spots, mostly because of the prohibitive cost of publishing large photographic collections. The ever more rapid rise of computer technology and Internet publication may soon solve these problems, however. There are already on-line catalogues to some of the more important air photographic libraries, which is a beginning. But it is to be hoped that before long the pictures themselves can be made available over the Web. High resolution, uncompressed digital images make for large computer files, but hard disc capacities have been growing exponentially in recent years, so that it is now possible to store many thousands of images on a single, relatively cheap, disc. High quality scanners are now available quite cheaply, and anyway it is probably only a matter of time before digital cameras become good enough to replace film for aerial use (albeit there are still doubts about the longevity of digital photographs). At present, one major barrier to the efficient use of large on-line photographic files is the pitifully slow speed of modem communications. But broader band alternatives are slowly becoming available and by the time this book has been in print for a few years the very idea of using a modem will probably appear laughably primitive. This will leave only copyright and revenue issues to surmount. If the collections concerned are to make their images available electronically, rather than selling prints, they will need to find alternative funding and/or charging structures if they are to continue their work and especially their flying programs.

In an area as well known as Hadrian's Wall there is always a danger of coming to believe that the current generation lies at some pinnacle of wisdom and knows the totality of the distribution of sites. If this book has a theme, however, it is that knowledge is never finite and our own is far from complete. Our understanding of the frontier and its history has grown out of all recognition over the last 100 years, but there is still a very long way to go. One thing, however, is certain and that is that aerial photography still has a major contribution to make.

Appendix
The anatomy of a Roman fort

This book spends much of its time describing the details of Roman forts as revealed in air photographs and although the main text makes free use of technical terms (some of which are in Latin), we are well aware that the general reader might find these a little bewildering. This appendix will thus provide a short guided tour of the layout of Roman forts, during which all will, hopefully, become clear.

First, let us define what we are discussing. The Roman army was divided into two basic groupings. The first were the legions. These were the Roman soldiers of popular imagination. They were elite, heavy infantry units of Roman citizens and were highly trained for both close formation fighting and as field engineers. Each legion was made up of 5,500 men, including a small, 120-strong, cavalry contingent, and they were based in huge fortresses of up to 60 acres in area. For most of the Roman period there were three legions based in Britain, *II Augusta*, *VI Victrix* and *XX Valeria Victrix*, but although these units build Hadrian's Wall, their fortresses lay well to the south in, respectively, Caerleon, York and Chester. This means that although these units were the backbone of the garrison of Britain, and the ultimate guarantors of the frontier's integrity, none of them were actually based on it.

The second grouping were known as auxiliaries. These were still highly trained men, but they were provincials, not Roman citizens, albeit they were led by Roman commanding officers holding the rank of Prefect or Tribune. They were also organised into much smaller units, of which there are a variety of types. Firstly, the auxiliaries provided most of Rome's cavalry, an arm with which Rome herself had never been especially successful. Cavalry units were called *Alae* (wings). *Alae* come in two types: *alae quingenaria*, and *alae milliaria*, which were 500 and 1,000 strong respectively. Milliary *alae* are extremely rare though. At present, only nine are known over the whole of the Roman Empire, of which just one was based in Britain.

The rest of the auxiliary troops were organised as cohorts, which again could be 500 or 1,000 strong. Most of them would be wholly made up of infantry, often of a lighter variety than the legions. But others are so-called *cohors equitata*, which were part mounted units in which about a third of the strength was cavalry. Finally, there were a few specialist units of archers and some amphibious specialists, such as the Batavians from the area around the Rhine delta. Auxiliary units, like the legions, usually had a name and a number, with the name generally giving the area or people from whom they were recruited. It was usual practice for the Roman army to post auxiliaries away from their homeland to lessen any danger of insurrection. This means that in Britain we find units such as *Ala I Hispanorum*, from Spain, or *Coh I Dacorum*, from Romania, whilst units of Britons are found elsewhere.

All of these units were based in forts of between three and nine acres in area and, as auxiliaries made up the entire garrison of Hadrian's Wall, it is to these bases that this appendix is directed.

It is often said that Roman forts were completely standardised, so that if we excavate any fort anywhere in the empire, we can expect to find exactly the same design. Indeed, in the past, excavators have been known to try to reconstruct an entire fort plan on the basis of just a few small slit trenches. In fact, however, this is a gross exaggeration. As yet, no identical Roman forts have been found. There can be considerable differences even between neighbouring forts which are obviously part of the same deployment. Nevertheless, they do tend to be variations on a relatively constant theme, so that it remains possible to discuss forts as a distinct class rather than having to deal with every single one as a totally different site type. That said, when we hunted through the published literature to find an excavated fort to stand as a typical example, we were unable to chose one. Our sample plan (**91**) is thus our own construct, although it is wholly made up of elements from a variety of real Roman forts (all from Hadrian's Wall). Most of the forts on the Wall were built of stone, but it is important to remember that many Roman forts have turf built defences and timber internal buildings, although this does not effect their overall layout.

The plan shows a small fort of three and a half to four acres such as might be occupied by a *cohors quingenaria* and the first thing that will be apparent is the distinctive shape of its defensive wall circuit. With only a tiny handful of exceptions, this is a rectangle with rounded corners. Some forts are nearly square, but on Hadrian's Wall the most common form is a playing card shape.

The rampart is pierced by four gates. These are usually divided by a central pier into two separate arched carriageways, and they are flanked by guard chambers, which usually carried towers above the level of the rampart walk. The gates in the fort's short axis are usually located centrally, but in the long axis they tend to be set about a third of the way along, thus dividing the fort into two unequal parts. The smaller section was called the *praetentura* and was the front of the fort, usually facing any likely enemy. The rearward section was called the *retentura*. Larger forts would also sometimes have two, much smaller, single carriageway postern gates two-thirds of the way down the long axis, but this is by no means a universal feature. In addition to the gates, the fort walls would generally have watchtowers at the corners and at intervals around the circuit and the fort would also be surrounded by one or more ditches, with entrance breaks facing the gateways.

Inside the fort, the buildings were laid out around a regular street grid. Firstly, there was a road around the entire interior of the defences, called the *intervallum*. Next was the fort's main street, or *Via Principalis*, which ran between the two long axis gates and separated the *praetentura* from the *retentura*. Lastly, apart from an assortment of alleys between buildings, was the *Via Praetoria*, which linked the centre of the *Via Principalis* with the front gate.

The forward part of the *retentura* was usually occupied by a group of four buildings, collectively known as the main range, strictly speaking this constitutes a third area known as the *latera praetorii* These all front onto the *Via Principalis* and fall into three types. The first (**91**, 1) is called the *Principia*. This was the fort's headquarters or administration block and it is generally divided into a number of distinct sections. At the front was an open courtyard, which sometimes contains a well, and which was flanked by a colonnade or by ranges of storerooms and offices. Behind this was a large, covered transverse hall. This formed an assembly area where courts martial and other formal events could be held and there was usually a platform, known as a tribunal, at one end, from which the commander could preside. Finally, at the rear of the building was a further range of offices, in the centre of which was a room set aside as a shrine called the *sacellum*. Here images of the gods and the Emperor could be kept, along with the unit's standards, which were

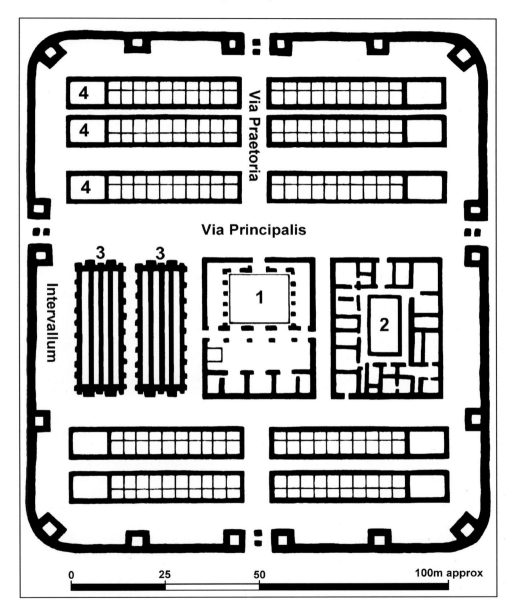

91   A typical Roman fort plan. DJW

themselves venerated as sacred. The garrison's cash reserves would also often be held here under guard, and a number of Hadrian's Wall forts have strong rooms constructed underneath this room. Occasionally, especially in cavalry forts, the *Via Principalis* would be roofed where it passed the *principia* to act as a covered exercise hall, and a number of such structures are known on the Wall.

Next to the *principia* was another large rectangular building known as the *praetorium* (**91**, 2). This was the commanding officer's residence and was a large, Mediterranean style, courtyard house in keeping with the standing of the commander, who would be a member of Rome's second rank aristocracy: the Equestrian Order. The houses could be very grand indeed (although smaller than their legionary equivalents) and may even have had second floors. They were relatively luxurious, often containing private bath suites and stables, as well as domestic areas, in which many of the rooms can have under floor heating. But the officer would have been present with his entire household, including slaves and horses, and may also have needed to perform diplomatic and other public functions at home in which it was important that he was able to impress.

The final standard element of the main range were the *horrea*, or granaries (**91**, 3), of which there were usually two. As their name suggests, these were food stores, although they probably held more than just grain. They were long rectangular buildings and their walls are instantly recognisable because they were supported by projecting buttresses to help their structure withstand extremely heavy loads. Their floors were supported well clear of the ground by lines of squat columns or low walls, to give some protection against vermin, and they had ventilation grills into the resulting substructure to allow air to circulate under the floor and ensure freedom from damp. At their front (and sometimes

92   A clavicula style temporary camp gate at Stracathro, Angus. DJW

rear) the granaries had stepped loading bays leading down to street level and some, at least, may have had porched entrances, to prevent rain blowing in when the doors were opened. Many forts have other buildings in their central areas, such as workshops (*fabricae*) and, in larger forts, even hospitals (*valetudinaria*), but these three types were the basic minimum and are encountered virtually everywhere.

The remainder of the fort, including most of the *praetentura*, was filled with barrack blocks (**91**, 4). The units were subdivided into centuries (*centuriae*), in the case of infantry, and *turmae* for cavalry, under the command of centurions and decurions respectively and each barrack block was designed to hold one of these groupings, as well as stabling the horses of the cavalry. Figure **91** shows an infantry fort and so the barracks are set up for centuries, but cavalry barracks are broadly similar in design. Each long block has a substantial area at the rampart end set aside for the officer and these were generally subdivided into rooms, although not to any particular standard plan. The remainder housed the men themselves and it is important to note that, contrary to logic, a century was a unit of 80 men and not 100. The block was thus divided into ten two-room units called *contubernia,* which each held an eight-man squad, who would also share a tent in the field. It is thought that equipment may have been kept in one room whilst the sleeping quarters were in the other, but this is not certain. One thing that is conspicuously lacking in Roman forts is a communal cooking and messing structure, so food would presumably have been eaten in the barracks. But there were usually ovens set into the ramparts so that the men could cook their rations without presenting too much of a fire or health risk to their accommodation.

In addition to its permanent forts, Hadrian's Wall also features large numbers of Roman temporary camps, and it was standard practice for the Roman army to build itself a fortified camp every night when operating in hostile territory. The first-century historian Josephus tells us how legions could construct a marching camp in three hours, and literally hundreds have now been located in Britain, mainly by aerial photography. These structures usually comprised a rampart built of earth and/or stacked turves, fronted by a V-shaped ditch. There are a number of telltale features that can identify them. They often have a regular shape, which is generally similar to that of a fort: a square or rectangle with rounded corners (although far more irregular examples are known). They also tend to show one of a number of distinctive entrance types. Camp builders did not have the time or materials to build proper gates, but the entrance gaps were often protected by short offset banks and ditches, just outside the camp, which were known as *tituli* (see **57 & 71**). Alternatively (although rare on the Wall), a *clavicula*, or half-moon shaped ditch (**92**, arrowed) curving towards the exterior (and/or, in rarer cases, the interior) can indicate the position of the entrance. In both cases the object was to force an attacker to try to approach the entrance at an angle from the left, so that his shield would be turned away, making him vulnerable to defensive fire from the camp. At their largest, camps of this kind in Britain range up to 145 acres in area. The great majority along Hadrian's Wall are far smaller, however, and probably represent construction (rather than campaigning) camps, built to provide security for personnel and stores during the building of the line. Others, especially the smallest, may represent training exercises. For it is known that the Roman army conducted drills in the building of camps, as it did with virtually every other military skill.

Bibliography

Abbreviations
RIB   Collingwood, R.G. and Wright, R.P. 1965, *The Roman Inscriptions of Britain*, Oxford

Ancient sources

Anon. The Scriptores Historiae Augustae
Anon. The Notitia Dignitatum
Josephus The Jewish Wars

Modern writers

Alston, R. 1995 Soldier and society in Roman Egypt, London
Austen, P.S 1991 'How big was the second largest fort on Hadrian's Wall at Bowness on Solway?', in Maxfield, V.A. and Dobson, M.J. (ed) Roman Frontier Studies 1989, Proceedings of the XVth International Congress of Roman Frontier Studies, Exeter, 6-8
Austen, P.S. 1991a Bewcastle and Old Penrith: a Roman outpost fort and a frontier vicus, excavations 1977-8, CWAAS Res Ser, 6, Kendal
Austen, P.S. 1994 'Recent excavations on Hadrian's Wall, Burgh-by-Sands', CW(2), 94, 35-54
Baradez, J. 1949 Fossatum Africae, Paris
Bellhouse, R.L. 1955 'The Roman Fort at Burrow Walls Near Workington', CW(2), 55, 30-45
Bellhouse, R.L. 1962 'Moricambe in Roman Times and Sites on the Cumberland Coast', CW(2), 62, 56-72
Bellhouse, R.L. 1969 'Roman Sites on the Cumberland Coast 1966-67', CW(2), 69, 79-101
Bellhouse, R.L. 1970 'Roman Sites on the Cumberland Coast 1968-1969', CW(2), 70, 9-47
Bellhouse, R.L. 1981 'Roman Sites on the Cumberland Coast : Milefortlet 20, Low Mire', CW(2), 81, 7-14
Bellhouse, R.L. 1981 'Hadrian's Wall: The Limiting Ditches in the Cardurnock Peninsula', Britannia, 12, 135-42
Bellhouse, R.L. 1989 Roman Sites on the Cumberland Coast, A New Schedule of Coastal Sites, Kendal
Bellhouse, R.L. 1992 Joseph Robinson of Maryport, archaeologist extraordinary, Otley
Bellhouse, R.L. and Richardson, G.G.S. 1975 'The Roman site at Kirkbride, Cumberland', CW(2), 58-90
Bellhouse, R.L. and Richardson, G.G.S. 1982 'The Trajanic Fort at Kirkbride; The Terminus Of The Stanegate Frontier', CW(2), 82, 35-50
Bidwell, P. 1999 Hadrian's Wall 1989-1999, Kendal
Bidwell, P. and Speak, S. 1994 Excavations at South Shields Roman fort, vol. 1, Newcastle

Birley, E.B. 1951 'The Roman fort and settlement at Old Carlisle', CW(2), 51, 16-39

Birley, E.B. 1961 Research on Hadrian's Wall, Kendal

Birley, E.B. and Bellhouse, R.L. 1963 'The Roman site at Kirkbride', CW(2), 63, 126-39

Bishop, M.C. and Dore, J.N. 1988 Corbridge, excavations of the Roman fort and town, 1947-80, London

Bowman, A.K. and Thomas, J.D. 1984 Vindolanda: The Latin Writing-tablets, Gloucester

Bowman, A.K. and Thomas, J.D. 1991 'A Military Strength Report From Vindolanda', J.R.S., 81, 62-73

Bowman, A.K. and Thomas, J.D. 1994 The Vindolanda Writing-tablets II, Dorchester

Breeze, D.J. 1972 'Excavations at the Roman Fort of Carrawburgh, 1967-1969', Arch Ael(4), 50, 87

Breeze, D.J. 1982 *The Northern Frontiers of Roman Britain*, London

Breeze, D.J. and Dobson, B. 2000 Hadrian's Wall, 4th ed, London

Capper, J.C. 1907 'Photographs of Stonehenge as seen from a war balloon', *Archaeologia*, 60, 571

Caruana, I.D. 1997 'Maryport and the Flavian Conquest of North Britain', in Wilson, R.J.A. (ed) *Roman Maryport and its Setting*, Nottingham 40 -51

Caruana, I.D. forthcoming *The Roman Forts at Carlisle: excavations at Annetwell Street, 1973-84*

Casey, P.J. and Savage, M. 1980 'Coins From the Excavations at High Rochester in 1852 and 1855', Arch Ael(5), 8, 75-88

Collingwood, R.G. 1930 'Hadrian's Wall a System of Numerical References', P.S.A.N.(4), 4, 179-87

Crow, J.G. 1987 'Peel Gap', Current Archaeology, 108, (Nov), 14

Crow, J.G. 1991 'A Review of Current Research on the Turrets and Curtain of Hadrian's Wall', Britannia, 22, 51-63

Crow, J.G. 1995 Housesteads, London

Dobson, B. 1986, 'The Function of Hadrian's Wall', Arch Ael(5), 14, 1-30

Frere, S.S. and St Joseph, J.K. 1983 Roman Britain from the Air, Cambridge

Gillam, J.P., Harrison, R.M. and Newman, T.G. 1973 'Interim Report on Excavations at the Roman Fort of Rudchester, 1972', Arch Ael(5), 1, 81-5

Groenman van Waateringe, W. 1980 'Urbanisation and the North West Frontier of the Roman Empire', in Hanson, W.S. and Keppie L.J.F. (ed) *Roman Frontier Studies 1979*, Oxford (Brit Arch Rep Int Ser, 71, vol 3), 1037-44

Groves, C. 1990 Tree-ring Analysis and Dating of Timbers From Annetwell Street, Carlisle, Cumbria, 1981-84, A.M. Lab Report 49/90, London

Haigh, D. and Savage, M. 1984 'Sewingshields', Arch Ael(5), 12, 33-148

Hartley, B.R. 1972 'The Roman Occupations of Scotland: The Evidence of Samian Ware', Britannia, 3, 1-55

Higham, N.J. and Jones, G.D.B., 1975 'Frontier, forts and farmers: Cumbrian aerial survey 1974-7', Arch J, 132, 16-53

Higham, N.J. and Jones, G.D.B., 1985 The Carvetii, Gloucester

Hobley, A.S. 1989 'The Numismatic Evidence for the Post-Agricolan Abandonment of the Roman Frontier in Northern Scotland', *Britannia*, 20, 69-74

Hodgson, N. 2000 'The Stanegate: a frontier rehabilitated', Britannia, 31, 11-22

Holbrook, N. and Speak, S. 1994 'Washing Well Roman fort, a transcription of the aerial photographs and an assessment of the evidence', Arbeia Journal, 3, 33-45

Holder, P.A. 1982 The Roman Army in Britain, London

Jarrett, M.G. 1976 Maryport, Cumbria: A Roman Fort and its Garrison. (C&W Extra Series 22), Kendal

Jarrett, M.G. 1994 'Non-Legionary Troops in Roman Britain', Britannia, 25, 35-78

Jobey, G. 1977 'Burnswark Hill Dumfriesshire', TDGNHAS, 53, 57-104

Jobey, I. 1979 'Housesteads Ware, a Frisian tradition on Hadrian's Wall', Arch Ael(5), 7, 127-43

Jones, G.D.B. 1976 'The Western Extension of Hadrian's Wall: Bowness to Cardurnock', Britannia, 7, 236-43

Jones, G.D.B. 1978 'Concept and Development in Roman Frontiers', Bull J. Rylands Library, 61, 115-44

Jones, G.D.B. 1982 'The Solway Frontier: Interim Report 1976-81', Britannia, 13, 283-98

Jones, G.D.B. 1991 'The Emergence of the Tyne Solway Frontier' in Maxfield, V.A. and Dobson, M.J. (ed) Roman Frontier Studies 1989, Proceedings of the XVth International Congress of Roman Frontier Studies, Exeter, 98-107

Jones, G.D.B. 1993 'Excavations on a Coastal Tower, Hadrian's Wall: Campfield Tower 2B, Bowness-on-Solway', Manchester Archaeological Bull, 8, 31-9

Kilbride-Jones, H.E. 1938 'Excavation of a native settlement at Milking Gap, Northumberland', Arch Ael(4), 15, 303-50

Körtüm, K. 1998 'Zur Datierung der römischen Militäranlagen im obergermanisch-rätischen Limes gebiet, Chronologische Untersuchungen anhand der Münzfunde', *Saalburg Jahrbuch*, 49, 5-65

Luttwak, E.N. 1976 The Grand Strategy of the Roman Empire, Baltimore

Mann, J.C. 1974 'The Frontiers of the Principate', ANRW, II, principat 1, Berlin, 508-33

McCord, N. and Jobey, G. 1971 'Notes on Air Reconnaissance in Northumberland and Durham II', Arch Ael(4), 49, 119-30

Millett, M. 1990 *The Romanization of Britain*, Cambridge

Poidebard, A. 1934 La Trace de Rome Dans le Désert de Syrie, Paris

Potter, T.W. 1979 Romans in NW England, (C&W Research series 1), Kendal

Poulter, J. 1998 'The Date of the Stanegate and a Hypothesis About the Manner and Timing of the Construction of Roman Roads in Britain', Arch Ael(5), 26, 49-58

Richardson, G.G.S. 1977 'A Romano-British Farmstead at Fingland, Cumberland', CW(2), 77, 53-60

Richmond, I.A. 1929 'Excavations on Hadrian's Wall in the Gilsland-Birdoswald-Pike hill sector, 1928', CW(2), 29, 303-38

Richmond, I.A. 1933 'The Tower at Gillalees Beacon', CW(2), 33, 241-45

Richmond, I.A. 1936 'Excavations at High Rochester and Risingham', Arch Ael(4), 13, 170-98

Richmond, I.A. 1940 'The Romans in Redesdale' in Northumberland County History Committee, A History of Northumberland, Newcastle upon Tyne, 63-154.

Richmond, I.A. and Hodgson, K.S. 1934 'Excavations at Castlesteads', CW(2), 34, 159-65

Robertson, A.S. 1957 An Antonine fort, an account of excavations carried out on the Antonine Wall on Golden Hill Duntocher, Dunbartonshire, Edinburgh

Selkirk, R. 1983 The Piercebridge Formula, Cambridge

Shotter, D.C.A. 2000 'Petillius Cerialis in Northern Britain'. Northern History, 36:2, 189-98

Simpson, F.G. 1913 'The fort on the Stanegate at Throp', CW(2), 13, 363-81

Simpson, F.G. 1930 'The Roman Fort at Newbrough', P.S.A.N.(4), 4, 163-65

Simpson, F.G. 1934a 'Boothby, Castle Hill', CW(2), 34, 154-5

Simpson, F.G. and Hodgson, K.S. 1947 'The coastal milefortlet at Cardurnock', CW(2), 47, 78-127

Simpson, F.G. and McIntyre, J. 1933 'Pike Hill', CW(2), 33, 271-74

Simpson, F.G. and Richmond, I.A. 1936 'The Roman fort on the Stanegate and other remains at Old Church Brampton', CW(2), 36, 172-82

Simpson, F.G., Richmond, I.A., Hodgson, K.S. and St Joseph,. J.K. 1936 'The Stanegate', CW(2), 36, 182-91

Simpson, F.G. and St Joseph, J.K. 1934 'Nether Denton', CW(2), 34, 152-54

Snape, M., P. Bidwell *et al.* 2002 'The Roman Fort at Newcastle-upon-Tyne' Arch Ael(5) extra volume 31

Stevens, C.E. 1966 The Building of Hadrian's Wall, Kendal

Taylor, D.J.A., Robinson, J. and Biggins, J.A. 2000 'A report on a geophysical survey of the Roman fort and vicus at Halton Chesters', Arch Ael(5), 28, 37-46

Topping, P. 1987 'A New Signal Station in Cumbria', Britannia, 13, 298-99

Welfare, H.G. 1974 'A cemetery at High Nook, Nether Denton', CW(2), 74, 14-17

Welfare, H.G. 2000 'Causeways, at milecastles, across the ditch of Hadrian's Wall', Arch Ael(5), 28, 13-26

Wilmott, A. 1997 Birdoswald, excavations of a Roman fort on Hadrian's Wall and its successor settlements: 1987-92, London

Wilson, D.R. 2001 Air Photo Interpretation for archaeologists, Stroud

Woodfield, C. 1965 'Six Turrets on Hadrian's Wall' Arch Ael(4), 43, 87-200

Woodfield, P. 1966 'Barcombe Hill, Thorngrafton', Arch Ael(4), 44, 71-8

Woolliscroft, D.J. 1988 'The Outpost System of Hadrian's Wall, An Outer Limes ?', British Archaeology, 6, (March/April), 22-5

Woolliscroft, D.J. 1989 (a) 'Signalling and the Design of Hadrian's Wall', Arch Ael(5), 17, 5-20

Woolliscroft, D.J. 1990 'Barron's Pike, Possible Roman Signal Tower', CW(2), 90, 280-81

Woolliscroft, D.J. 2001 Roman Military Signalling, Stroud

Woolliscroft, D.J. forthcoming (a), 'Roman sites on the Antonine Wall at Garnhall, Cumbernauld', Proc Soc Antiq Scot

Woolliscroft, D.J. forthcoming (b) The Roman Frontier on the Gask Ridge, Perth & Kinross, TAFAC Monograph 3

Woolliscroft, D.J. and Jones, G.D.B. forthcoming Excavations at Silloth and Fingland Rigg on the Cumbrian Coast

Woolliscroft, D.J., Nevell, M.D. and Swain, S.A.M. 1989 'The Roman Site on Grey Hill, Bewcastle, Cumbria', CW(2), 89, 69-76

Woolliscroft, D.J. and Swain, S.A.M. 1991 'The Roman 'Signal' Tower at Johnson's Plain, Cumbria', CW(2), 91, 19-30

Woolliscroft, D.J., Swain, S.A.M. and Lockett, N.J. 1992 'Barcombe B, A Second Roman 'Signal Tower' on Barcombe Hill', Arch Ael (5), 20, 57-62

Useful websites

http://www.hadrians-wall.org/ (General site on Hadrian's Wall)

http://www.northumberland.gov.uk/vg/romans.html (General site on Hadrian's Wall)

http://museums.ncl.ac.uk/archive/ (The Museum of Antiquities of Newcastle Upon Tyne)

http://www.vindolanda.com/ (For Vindolanda fort)

http://uknets.8m.com/history.htm (For Wallsend fort)

http://www.brampton.co.uk/birdoswald/ (For Birdoswald fort)

http://www.roman-britain.org/hw/hw_menu.htm (General site for Roman Britain)

http://www.morgue.demon.co.uk/Britannia.html (For the Roman army and fortifications general)

http://home.t-online.de/home/bernd.hummel/awengl.htm (For the Antonine Wall)

http://www.morgue.demon.co.uk/Pages/Gask/ (For the Gask Frontier)

http://www.hunterian.gla.ac.uk/HuntMus/romans (The Hunterian Museum on Roman Scotland)

Index

Agache, R., 17
Agricola's, 26, 27, 82
Ala Augusta ob Virtutem Appellata, 72, 94
Ala Gallorum Sebosiana, 62
Ala I Hispanorum Asturum, 88
Ala I Pannoniorum Sabiniana, 93
Ala II Asturum, 95
Ala Petriana, 117
Amphitheater, 101
Annexes, 55, 65, 84, 142
Antenociticus (God), 80
Antonine Wall, 18, 25, 52, 71, 82-8, 96, 105, 119, 142, 144
Antoninus (Emperor), 18, 81, 87
Aqueducts, 40, 41, 45, 95, 106, 108, 109
Ardoch fort, 12, 28, 29
Artillery platforms, 138, 144
Augustus (Emperor), 21, 22, 24

Balloon photography, 16
Balmuildy fort, 82, 83
Bar Hill fort, 52
Baradez, J., 17
Barcombe towers, 37, 45-6
Barracks, 29, 47, 59, 71, 78, 80, 87, 88, 89, 94, 97, 98, 101, 108, 111, 124, 129, 137, 151
Barron's Pike tower, 135, 141
Baths, 41, 44, 45, 55, 79, 80, 89, 94, 95, 97, 99, 119, 129, 132, 139, 140, 141, 150
Beckfoot fort, 71, 128-31
Benwell fort, 80, 91, 112
Bewcastle fort, 111, 135, 139-42
Birdoswald fort, 80, 110-14, 117, 119, 139, 141
Birrens fort, 135, 139, 142-3

Boudicca, 26
Bowness-on-Solway fort, 76, 118, 120-2
Braasch, O., 17
Bradley, E., 16
Bridges, 18, 79, 89, 90, 94, 95, 108, 110, 111
Burgh-by-Sands fort, 35-7, 62-5, 70, 118-20
Burnswark, 143
Burrow Walls fort, 134
Bywell possible fort, 34

Caerleon, 87, 147
Caesar, Julius, 21, 24
Caratacus, 26
Cargill fortlet, 37
Carlisle, 19, 26, 34-8, 52, 60-2, 70-2, 95, 117, 118
Carrawburgh fort, 76, 92, 96-8, 100, 106
Carriden fort, 81
Cartimandua, 26
Carvoran fort, 33, 35, 36, 48-52, 59, 76, 110, 111, 115, 116, 120, 141
Castlecary fort, 82, 83
Castlehill Boothby fortlet, 33, 57
Castlesteads fort, 114-17, 120, 126, 142
Cemeteries, 56, 95, 110
Cerialis, 26, 62
Chalet barracks, 89, 98, 100, 108, 137
Chester, 40, 87, 147
Chesterholm fort, see Vindolanda
Chesters fort, 79-80, 94-7, 106, 110, 112
Chew Green, 139
Churches, 80
Claudius (Emperor), 21, 24, 81
Cocidius (God), 140, 142
Coh I Aelia Dacorum, 113, 139

Coh 1 Aelia Hispanorum, 142
Coh I Baetasiorum, 133
Coh I Batavorum, 97
Coh I Cornoviorum, 89
Coh I Dalmatarum, 95, 133, 138
Coh I Frisiaunum, 92, 97
Coh I Hamiorum Sagittaria, 52
Coh I Hispanorum, 29, 133
Coh I Lingonum, 120, 138
Coh I Nervana Germanorum, 118, 142
Coh I Tungrorum, 35, 44, 97, 100
Coh I Ulpia Traiana Cugenorum, 89, 97
Coh I Vangionum, 95, 137
Coh I Vardullorum, 93, 138
Coh II Asturum, 110
Coh II Dalmatarum, 56
Coh II Lingonum, 135
Coh II Nerviorum, 88
Coh II Pannoniorum, 128
Coh II Thracum, 135
Coh II Tungrorum, 115, 142
Coh III Batavorum, 35
Coh III Nerviorum, 44, 133
Coh IV Gallorum, 44, 115, 137
Coh IV Lingonum, 88
Coh V Gallorum, 88
Coh VI Nerviorum, 110
Coh VI Raetorum, 110
Coh VII Batavorum, 35
Coh IX Batavorum, 44
Contubernia, 78, 88-9, 98, 100, 151
Corbridge, 19, 34-41, 48, 62
Coventina (Goddess), 97
Crawford, O.G.S., 16
Crop marks, 7, 13-15, 17, 19, 27, 28, 38, 54, 55, 57, 66, 127, 131, 137, 145
Croy Hill fort, 83
Cumberland coast milefortlets:
  MF 1, 122-3, 125, 127
  MF 5, 124-6, 134
  MF 9, 125-6, 134
  MF 12, 127
  MF 17, 131
  MF 23, 131
  MF 27 (possible), 134

Cumberland coast towers:
  TR 2b, 123-4
  TR 4b, 123
  TR 14b, 128, 130
  TR 26b, 134
Cuneus Frisiorum, 100

Dacia, 24
Dalswinton fort, 14, 32, 36
Danube frontier, 13
Dere Street, 32, 39-41, 92-4, 109, 135, 137, 139
Digital photographs, 146
Domitian (Emperor), 26, 31, 52
Doune fort, 27
Drumburgh fort, 118, 120, 123, 130
Drumquhassle fort, 27
Duntocher fort, 82-4

Easton tower, 70
Edward I, 35, 62, 127

Farhill tower, 68-70
Fingland Rigg, 68-71

Garnhall tower, 71, 83
Gask frontier, 7, 18, 20, 27-32, 36, 37, 46, 63, 78, 83
German frontier, 25, 27, 143
Gillalees Beacon tower, 135, 141
Glenbank fortlet, 29-31
Granaries, 40, 47, 59, 64, 87, 88, 90, 98, 112, 129, 137, 150, 151
Great Chesters fort, 89, 101, 104, 106-10
Greenloaning tower, 31
Grey Hill settlement, 140
Grindon Hill possible fortlet, 34

Hadrian (Emperor), 18, 26, 47, 75, 80, 81
Halton Chesters fort, 92-4
Haltwhistle Burn fortlet, 33, 42, 47-8, 52-3, 57, 59, 78, 105
Hardknott fort, 133
High Crosby possible fortlet, 33

High Rochester fort, 109, 135-9
Hillforts, 42, 46, 139, 143, 144
Hospitals, 88, 98
Hostage taking, 44
Housesteads fort, 79, 84, 89, 98-101, 104, 133

Inchtuthil fortress, 27
Insall, G.S.M., 16

Jarrow possible fort, 34

Kaims Castle fortlet, 29-30
Kirkbride fort, 34-5, 66-70, 130, 132
Kirkby Thore fort, 49
Kite photography, 8
Knag Burn gate, 99, 101

Latrine, 98
Lautertal, 13
Legionary compounds, 40, 41, 62
Lilia, 85, 88
Limestone Corner, 85-6, 95-6
Local government in vici, 80
Loudon Hill fort, 32

Maiden Way, 48, 139
Mains Rigg tower, 37, 56, 114, 141
Mansiones, 45, 80
Marcus Aurelius (Emperor), 81-2
Maryport fort, 121, 125, 130-4
Masada, 144
Midgate fortlet, 29, 31
Milecastles:
  MC 19, 93
  MC 29, 95
  MC 30, 85, 96
  MC 34, 91
  MC 35, 97, 101
  MC 37, 101-2
  MC 38, 104-5
  MC 39, 101-2
  MC 40, 101, 104
  MC 41, 104
  MC 42, 77-8, 80, 101-2, 105

MC 44, 110
MC 45, 108, 110
MC 46, 51, 110
MC 48, 78, 110
MC 49, 110-11
MC 50 TW, 114
MC 51, 113, 114
Military Way, 85, 87, 95-7, 99, 102, 104,
  111, 118, 128, 129
Milking Gap settlement, 104-5
Milton fort, 32
Mithraea, 80, 92, 97, 99
Mons Graupius, 26
Moresby fort, 133-4
Moricambe, 34, 66, 124-5, 134
Muir O' Fauld tower, 29-30

Nero (Emperor), 26
Nerva (Emperor), 31, 142
Nether Denton fort, 33, 35-7, 54-9, 111-
  12, 114
Netherby fort, 135, 141-2
Newbrough, 34, 41-3, 53
Newcastle, 19, 39, 52, 76, 88-91, 97
Newstead fort, 32, 36
Notitia Dignitatum, 92-3, 95, 97, 100, 120,
  133, 135, 137
Numeri Exploratorum, 135, 137-9, 142
Numerus Hnaudifridi, 100

Old Carlisle fort, 70-3, 94-5
Old Church Brampton fort, 33, 37, 58-9,
  114
Old Kilpatrick fort, 82
Osterburken fort, 143

Papcastle fort, 118
Parade grounds, 99, 133
Parthian Empire, 24
Peel Gap tower, 102, 104
Pennymuir, 139
Pervensey fort, 137
Pike Hill tower, 37, 56
Poidebard, A., 16

Portgate, 92, 94
Praetoria, 34, 40, 44, 59, 87, 88, 94, 98, 112, 150
Principiae, 40, 44, 59, 64, 87, 88, 90, 94, 98, 106, 112, 129, 139, 142, 148, 150

Ravenglass fort, 121, 134
Reconstructions, 45, 89, 94, 110
Red House, 38-9
Risingham fort, 135, 137-8
Roman Gask Project, 7, 20, 31
Rough Castle fort, 83-5
Round houses, 44, 106
Rudchester fort, 91-2, 97

Sacellum, 149
Severus (Emperor), 87, 112
Shadow marks, 13, 15, 92, 145
Shielhill South tower, 31
Siege works, 139, 143-4
Signalling, 30, 37-8, 46, 70, 114, 119, 135, 141
Silloth, 127-9
Soil marks, 15-16, 28
Somme Valley, 16
South Shields fort, 34, 87-9
St.Joseph, J.K., 17-18, 57, 95, 126
Stables, 88-9, 150
Stainmore, 49
Stanwix fort, 62, 117-18, 133, 141
Stracathro fort and camp, 27, 150
Strageath fort, 28, 31
Strip buildings, 41, 45, 95
Strong rooms, 94, 106, 108

Temple, 40, 45, 80, 92, 97, 99, 140
Temporary camps, 13, 42, 51-2, 64, 66-7, 96, 104, 107, 109, 118, 120, 130, 139, 144, 150-1
Thirwall Gap, 48, 51-2
Throp fortlet, 33, 52-7, 59
Titus (Emperor), 26
Tombs, 107, 109
Training areas, 139, 144

Trajan (Emperor), 24, 27, 34, 37, 47, 75, 89
Turf Wall, 76, 78, 111-15, 119, 123
Turrets:
 T 13b, 92
 T 29b, 85
 T 34b, 99
 T 35a, 78, 97
 T 48a, 110
 T 48b, 109-10
 T 49a, 112
 T 49b, 110, 113-14
 T 50b TW, 114

Vallum, 18, 49, 51-2, 77, 80-1, 84-5, 88-9, 92, 95-7, 99, 105-6, 114, 116, 118, 122
Varus, 24
Venutius, 26
Vespasian (Emperor), 26
Veterans, 80
Vexillatio Raetorum Gaesatorum, 137
Vici, 44-5, 52, 55-6, 62, 73, 79-80, 84, 89-90, 92, 95, 97, 99-100, 108, 112, 116, 118, 129, 133, 137-8, 140-2, 145
Vindolanda fort, 33-6, 38, 41, 43-7, 49, 59, 62, 95, 97, 137, 143

Wallsend fort, 76, 78, 88-9, 91-2, 94, 98, 142
Washing Well Whickam fort, 34-6, 38-9
Water mills, 79
Whin Sill, 18, 76, 78-9, 97, 101
Whitley Castle fort, 49
Wilderness Plantation fortlet, 83
Wing walls, 82, 110
Women, 35, 79-80, 138
Wooden Law hillfort, 139, 144
Writing tablets, 34, 44, 62

York, 40, 87, 147